MY POSITIVE FACE
OF DISFIGUREMENT

A True Story

BY

DAVID BIRD

Author's Dedication

This book is dedicated to my Mother and my late Father who
have been the most loving and caring of parents; through all
the heartache that was associated with my disablement and
disfigurement they were always there to make sure that I
was provided for and looked after. To Joanne my wife, who
accepted me for the person I was inside and not for what I
looked like, the love given to me has lasted through all our
years together and finally to another very special person in
my life, my very dearest daughter Lindsay, our only child but
a gift from God.

I love you all.

Acknowledgements

There are many people that I would like to acknowledge, who have helped me during the course of producing this book, and there are also many others who came into my life through other ways, for this I am truly thankful. No doubt, during the course of compiling this list I will undoubtedly miss someone out, it's purely due to the fact that my memory is not as good as it used to be. For those people that I have missed, thank you from the bottom of my heart, you have all made such an impact on my life. Please accept my sincere apologies for this, I am truly sorry

Ian S G Smith. Dental Surgeon. Ian helped me to build my self-confidence, without him I don't think I would be the person that I am today. James Partridge. CEO Changing Faces. James gave me several opportunities to be involved with media work for the charity, yet another man who taught me self-belief, Professor Geoffrey Rose. and Professor John Wright Ophthalmic Consultant Surgeons. For all the help that they gave me to me over many years regarding my medical condition. They both made my life more bearable. Godfrey Sturgeon. Engine List Compiler. Many thanks must go to this wonderful old gentleman for the help he gave in collating the list of traction engines once owned by Henry and Arthur Bird.

MY POSITIVE FACE
OF DISFIGUREMENT

A True Story

BY

DAVID BIRD

Author's Note

This is an account of my wonderful life story of learning to cope with a very rare congenital condition, of my happy childhood and the trials and tribulations of my teenage years and adult days.

SOMETHING

I'm a Norfolk Beauty a canary throu and throu

Here's a little something I'm gonn'a tell you

I've got something rather precious something quite unique

Come a little closer boy! I'll take my tongue in cheek

It's something I was given in a very special way

It's something I will treasure till my dying day

It's something I was born with something you can't see

It's something you will recognize something tis only me

It's my well known Norfolk accent which I treasure o so dear

But while I have a Norfolk tongue I'll take it everywhere

Jill Tann

In Loving Memory Of Jill

2016

CONTENTS

ANCESTRAL ROOTS

As I've grown older and the years have flown by, I have felt a desperate need to learn of my ancestral roots; a yearning to search for my history of where I and my forbears came from. In this search I have been taken to several corners of the British Isles in order to gain this information.

I remember as a little lad asking my late grandfather (Ted) Cecil Sutton where his family came from. My grandfather told me that he was born in a public house called The Carpenters Arms in East Winch; this is a village near King's Lynn in Norfolk. He said that his father Roland Tom was born in Bolton in Lancashire. Grandad went on to tell me that his own grandfather was Frank, and that he also came from Lancashire. The information that my grandfather gave me was to be the beginning of my family research!

From my little talk with Grandad I had made myself a promise that one day I would perhaps try to find out more about my family history. This was something that I decided I had to do way back in the late 1960's. Now one fact that you must realise is that all those years ago it was rather a difficult proposition actually to find out any of your own history, because most of the records were held in archives and could only be accessed by professional researchers, or family historians as they may well be known. In actual fact you would probably have had to employ a certified genealogist, a professional person, to research your history for you.

Several years went by and this yearning to know more about my ancestors grew stronger, until one day in 2003 I acquired my first computer. This opened the floodgates for me to begin my research. Over a period of years I have been able to acquire some of that ancestral history. The small pieces of information that my late Grandad initially gave me have at last enabled me to find out more about my family members from past times.

I did a preliminary search in the Census of 1901 to hunt for my Sutton family, and found most of grandfather's brothers and sisters living at East Winch, as he had first told me all those years ago. Having studied this information, I decided to send for Grandad's birth certificate. Within two or three weeks the certificate had arrived with all of the details, including his parents' names and their occupations of the day. This brilliant little snippet of family history really got me hooked and I found myself wanting to know more. I continued my search by sending for the certificates of the marriage of my great-grandparents and also the birth of my great-grandfather Roland Tom.

My investigations went even further and I soon found that Roland Tom did not come from Lancashire as my grandfather had stated, but had actually been born in a small village in Wiltshire called Brinkworth. I hadn't queried my grandfather's words all those years ago, but firmly believed that my roots did in fact begin in Lancashire. To my astonishment I was surprised to find out this new information. The marriage certificate did indeed say that Frank was my great-grandfather's name, but on Roland

Tom's birth certificate it stated that his father's name was Thomas Sutton and his mother was Susannah (formerly Hathway). Why would my grandfather have been led into thinking that his roots were in Lancashire, when his grandfather and the whole of that family had originated in the county of Wiltshire? This is one of life's great mysteries and we'll probably never know unless new information turns up.

Another query that entered my head was that I just couldn't understand why this family had left the county of Wiltshire and moved hundreds of miles away! This had played on my mind for quite some time up until just a few months ago. I happened to come across a family history magazine, and there before me was the answer to this riddle that was written in black and white. I found that by the late 1870's hundreds people migrated northwards in search of work, some even migrating to other countries. Several members of my Sutton clan did this too and travelled further up-country to Lincolnshire. The main reason for this move was that agricultural trends were on a downturn, especially in Wiltshire and the surrounding counties, they were in desperate need of work to survive. These were large families and without doing something as drastic as this they would have been in absolute poverty, and so this particular family ended up in a new county far from their beloved homes. I would imagine that it would have been quite a frightening prospect for all concerned not knowing how their futures would turn out to be.

On looking at the Census of 1881 for Somerby in Lincolnshire I found Roland Tom along with his father, mother, brother and sisters living in Granville Street near to Grantham. What an incredible change from the beautiful rolling hills of Wiltshire to the very flat lands of this new county! Having found this, I started to delve even deeper and determined that I should look for more information relating to Wiltshire. I then decided to go back to the 1871 Census; in this search I found the whole of this family were living in a Manor House at a place called Winterbourne Gunner. Thomas was listed as being an assistant farmer.

Since doing this search I've now found that Wiltshire has quite a few of my ancestors. There seems to have been a large group of Suttons living in this county, especially in and around the Brinkworth area. I have been very lucky in the fact that I was able to use our local family history centre in King's Lynn and sent for the microfiche reels relating to the Parish Registers of Brinkworth; these registers contain several members of the Sutton family.

Here are just a few of my forebears that I've managed to track down:- John & Sarah Sutton were my 6 x great grandparents; they had a son John who was born in 1744. John was baptised on 26th August of that same year. John married Hannah Hedges in Brinkworth on 21st May 1770, and followed in his father's footsteps by becoming a yeoman farmer; this was a tenant farmer who probably rented just a few acres of land and possibly owned some livestock. It would appear that several of my Sutton ancestors were yeoman, and just recently I've received a document from the

Wiltshire and Swindon Archives stating that James Sutton, my 4 x great-grandfather took on the commission of Captain in the Wiltshire Yeomanry; the actual document is signed by King George III and dated 21st June 1794, and by early 1797 he had been made up to Lieutenant Colonel. These yeomanry farmers/soldiers would have been like the Territorial Army of today, those men could have been called up at any time to protect their country. I am so proud of these links, and through finding this wonderful history. I also know that we had seven of my direct descendants from my grandfather, going way back through to my 6 x great-grandfather John Sutton, all of them being farmers way back into the early 1700's. I've now received further documents from the Wiltshire Archives relating to the history of the Suttons, one of them being James's will and the other regarding the lands that he had farmed.

You know, it's very strange, I've been down to Wiltshire a few times in my life and I've always felt that it was somewhere that I might have belonged to, even to the extent of the feeling those pre-history links that we hear about from this beautiful part of the country, and they lie deep in my veins. I am really drawn to this county!

I have tried so desperately hard to research my Bird line, but up to this present time of writing I have unfortunately only been able to trace my 2 x great-grandfather, Henry Bird, who was born about 1794 near Attleborough in Norfolk. Henry married Mary Doubleday and she came from Besthorpe, a small hamlet about 8 miles just south-west of Wymondham. Henry and Mary married in

Beothorpe on 20th January 1816 and they had four children:-
Marianne 1816, Thomas 1824, Robert 1826 and of course
Henry my great-grandfather, who was born in 1833. This had
been a very poor family as most of the older children along
with their father were listed as labourers in some documents
that I've found.

From the research that I did of the census
information, Henry seems to have been a person who really
wanted something better out of life. In the records of 1851
and up until 1861 he had also been a labourer, but by 1871
he was listed as a machine owner. It seems as if Henry must
have worked very hard, as he had started his threshing
machine business. Apparently, he had been in partnership
with a man by the name of Samuel Dixon, but this enterprise
had been dissolved in 1868. This information had been
stated in one of Norfolk's newspapers of the time.

What exactly happened we'll never know, perhaps
there had been a disagreement of some description, maybe it
was something to do with money. Whilst looking into this
joint venture, I feel that it couldn't have lasted too long
because of what had been found in the census records. In
those few short years it had shown Henry's status, from
being just a labourer to a machine man, this was a wonderful
achievement, especially in those times.

From other information that I had acquired it was
very likely that Henry would probably been the owner of a
portable steam engine, thereby giving him an advantage over

others, this enabled him to work the land far quicker and easier than people of earlier years.

Henry and Hannah Lincoln, both aged twenty years were married on 8th April 1854 at Attleborough, and their first child, Edward, was born on 31st July of that same year. Unfortunately Edward only lived for just a few weeks and died on 5th October 1854. It wasn't until twelve years later in 1866 that Clara, their daughter was born. In the Census 1881 Henry was living with Hannah and Clara at the farm house in Vicarage Road in Great Hockham. Hannah lived for only three more years dying at the age of forty eight at Great Ellingham, her birth place.

By the 24th January 1886 Henry aged fifty three years old had married Elizabeth Brett my great-grandmother. Just as a matter of interest, Elizabeth was twenty four although on their wedding certificate it just stated, 'Of Full Age'. Arthur, my grandfather, was born on 3rd October of that year and my great aunt, Ellen Maud, was born in 1889.

So these were my ancestors, my links back to the past, a firm link to farming, especially on the Sutton side of my family.

THE EARLY YEARS

My own story starts in the Brecklands of Norfolk. Obviously my parents were from that wonderful farming background. My grandfather Arthur Bird was a threshing machine proprietor and would travel round the area of Great Hockham, threshing the corn for farmers. My mother's father, Ted, had a small farmstead called Heath Farm. He would buy and sell cattle, sheep and pigs, slaughter his own livestock for food, he also farmed some arable land.

Arthur had been in business with his father up until 1911, but when Henry died it was handed down to my grandfather. In Henry's will it stated that Arthur would have the business, and was left the great sum of £426:10 Shillings, but it also stated in the will that he would have to support his mother for the rest of her life by giving her 10 shillings a week. Elizabeth, my great-grandmother, lived for another thirty two years and died at the ripe old age of 81; this must have been a grand sum of money that had to be found on a weekly basis in order to keep his mother as Henry had wished! By around 1940 my father had also been taken into partnership with Arthur.

The farm at Great Hockham was quite big; there were several buildings around this yard where in its heyday my grandfather and his father before him ran the threshing machine business. There were all sorts of tools and equipment in his workshops which I seem to remember investigating as a little lad, it was like an Aladdin's cave. Grandfather's business ended in the early 1950's as the combine harvester was brought into the country, the need for threshing machines and traction engines came to a sad end, not only for him but for many others too.

Most of grandfather's threshing tackle and traction engines were cut up in his yard by scrap dealers for a mere few pounds. The finish of this enterprise must have been a very sad day for Grandfather, it had been a very prosperous business in the early days, and the success had made him a very wealthy man. Both he and his father before him had employed several labourers in the village of Great Hockham. In their time, they had owned some ten or eleven traction engines, most of these had come from Charles Burrell's at Thetford with an odd one or two that were from Garrett's and Ransome's Sims & Jefferies. (***Please see the engine list at the back of this book***).

My parents had been living with my grandparents at the farm in Great Hockham, but due to this loss of his business my father had to find another job. Luckily he found employment in the next village of Breckles where he started working for another local farmer, and they were also given a roof over their heads.

After a few months went by my mother, father and Chris, my elder brother, had moved from the village of Breckles to a remote smallholding called Watering Farm, which was out in the Brecklands in the Norfolk. This was about three miles from anywhere down an old dirt track road in the heart of the Brecklands countryside. Mum was expecting her 2nd child (me). They had been asked by her brother Elliott and his wife Dora if they would like to stay there with them until they could find a house in one of the nearby villages. My parents took up this offer and so moved to Watering Farm with Elliott and his family.

I was born at the farm On 23rd March 1954, second son to Gwen and Frank. My mother told me that it had been a difficult pregnancy, and when the time was getting near for me to arrive, Midwife Bennett was called in and had to cycle from the village of Rockland, this was over 6 miles away. Mother said that when she arrived, the midwife had been suffering from a bilious attack. This elderly lady must have been in some sort of agony as she went to lie on the bed alongside of mother. Apparently the old girl had fallen asleep and was snoring. My mother told me that the midwife had slept for quite a while, only to be woken by my father and Dora knocking on the bedroom door to see if everything was all right. The day progressed and I eventually arrived at around 1pm on Tuesday 23rd March. In those early days being born at home was the usual order of the day, and going into hospital to have your children was not really heard of.

Unfortunately I was born with a condition known as a vascular anomaly; this condition affects the right side of my head, face, eye, and mouth. This must have been a terrible shock for my parents at the time and took them by surprise. This problem makes my eye much larger than it should be because of an enlarged orbit (the bone structure around the eye). My head, face, eye and mouth have abnormal veins which are affected quite badly when I bend or over exert myself, and this has lead to several problems for me throughout my life. I was, however, healthy in myself and over the next few months progressed quite well; in fact I even remember Mother once saying to me in later years that I had always been the better child out of the three boys to feed. After a few months living at Watering Farm a small house came up for rent in the village of Thompson, so my parents decided that it would be good to idea to move, and this was to be where I grew up and spent most of my early childhood.

We moved to Well Corner, a small thatched cottage near to the village centre, this was within easy walking distance of the school, local shop and post office. We were now living within a small community, somewhere that we could at least be in touch with more people, friends and family and not miles from anywhere. My mum and dad were of course thankful to Elliott and Dora for their kindness and the help that had been given to them in the time they were at Watering Farm, but it was also good that my parents had a place of their own to live in. The little house was lovely and we all soon settled down in this beautiful little village, a place that I grew to love so dearly.

I was obviously just a baby of only a few months old when we moved into the rural community, people would soon get used to seeing me about and the disfigurement that I was born with. As far as everyone who came into contact with me were concerned, I was David, just a normal child like anybody else's offspring.

HOSPITAL VISITS

From just a few months old I started going to hospital, and this has been a major part of my life. I attended a clinic at the Norfolk & Norwich Hospital and the Jenny Lind Children's Hospital, also at Norwich. At one time I was admitted to the Norfolk & Norwich for tests, as the consultants were concerned about my condition. I stayed in the hospital for about a week, but the circumstances were not as they feared so, as you now realise, this problem has been with me all of my life. On that particular visit to the hospital my mother had said that she was so frightened to leave me because of a little lad who had been in one of the children's wards for several weeks. The nurses had spoilt this little boy so much, and for him to see a baby of only a few months old being fussed over was more than he could handle - he was just so jealous. My mother insisted that they watch over me very carefully in case the little lad tried to hurt me in any way; apparently he was poking his fingers into me in the cot. The worry for my mother was unthinkable, but nothing became of this and my stay in hospital soon ended.

Every year I continued to visit the hospital. My consultant was Mr Beatie; he was always such a nice old chap and even offered to try and help! He decided that he had an idea that they would stitch up the corner of my eye to make it look smaller, but this idea was soon dismissed as they feared that it would cause more problems than I was experiencing already. As a child I had never been allowed to go to the dentist but I remember very vividly going to the Jenny Lind Children's Hospital for any treatment that I needed. The major issue was that these large veins that I had on my eye were also on my head and in my mouth, surgery in any shape or form was quite a chief concern for both my parents and the doctors.

I once had to have a tooth removed and my father took me to the Jenny Lind. I was given anaesthetic and gas to put me to sleep while the extraction took place. I came round feeling terribly groggy but they decided that they would let my Dad take me home in the car. All the way home I was drifting in and out of sleep; the anaesthetic and gas had taken longer to leave my system than was intended. I kept hearing my father's voice. It was as if he was in the very far distance calling my name, and I remember him doing this all of the journey home! He just kept asking me if I was all right and whether I felt OK. I think he must have been very worried, as he thought that I wasn't going to come round and out of this very well.

A few days after this event he told me that he would never take me home from hospital again after having something done - or at least until after I had fully recovered. I know that it really frightened my father to see me like this. Over the next few years and up until my late teens I attended the Norfolk & Norwich and the Jenny Lind, but cannot even imagine how many visits I must have made in those early years.

Both my mum and dad had been there for me whenever I had to be at the hospitals, the worry for them

both must have been dreadful, what a terrible burden to
carry all of their lives

MUM & DAD

I know that most children would say that their parents were really wonderful people and that they couldn't have wished for anyone better. This must be true for most children, obviously it was no exception for me either. My parents have been what I could only describe as the best; to think what they had to put up with throughout the whole of my childhood, it must have been a dreadful worry for them both. I can only say that they must have been very strong in mind and spirit in order to have coped with me, and my medical condition all of their lives, even up to this day my mother still worries over me.

I have of course tried to lead a life which has been as near to normal as I possibly could. I've done lots of things throughout my lifetime that could have caused me some major issues to my medical condition, but the thought of whether I was doing right or wrong never entered into my mind. My parents worries over those sorts of happenings always seemed so unfounded to me. The years have gone by and of course we now have a family of our own so fully understand how much parents can worry. Both Joanne and I realise what it's like to be concerned over our daughter. As you can imagine, it must have been far worse for both our families, especially with me being disabled, and of course Joanne having been born deaf.

Unfortunately in January 1997 my Dad died, having suffered from emphysema. Dad had endured this illness for quite some time and to see him trying to get his breath was so saddening. I think that this illness came along because of all of his years of smoking, it may have also been the environment that he had been living in, pubs were notorious for being smoke filled places. It's a well known fact that breathing fumes from other smokers can dramatically cause this problem too.

I remember that he gave up cigarettes about two years before he died, but this was far too late to save him from this terrible disease. At least his suffering has ended, but I do wish he was still here with us, I do miss him so badly. It's been over 19 years now, but there are not many days when he's not here in my mind. I know my mother misses him so much too, but she's always been very positive and is still a wonderful mother, she still worries over us all. I know she will never ever change from being that special Mum, who has always cared for me so much throughout my life. She will be 89 years old in September, she really is such a remarkable woman for her age, she still cooks a wonderful meal when we turn up to see her.

I know that the day my father died played on my mind for weeks and weeks after! Joanne and I had made an arrangement to go away that particular weekend. I think we were off to Bournemouth or somewhere similar, down south anyway. Mum and Dad had agreed to have our daughter Lindsay for us that particular weekend, we were going to drop her off on the Friday afternoon when I had finished work. I had phoned my parents on the Thursday evening to make sure all was OK for them to have her, Mum said it would be fine.

I went to work on Friday morning as normal but couldn't wait to get finished, we hadn't been on a break from home in such a long time. We journeyed over to Middleton, to where Mum and Dad lived. We walked in the bungalow, and as soon I saw my Dad, I realised that something was desperately wrong; he looked so ashen faced and ill. I asked Mum if the Doctor had been in to see him and she said that he had visited earlier that morning. I was very worried by the way my father was looking and so telephoned their surgery to see if somebody could come out to him. It must have been about an hour later when the doctor arrived. He examined my Dad and said that he had pneumonia and that it might be a good idea to get him into hospital. Dad wasn't too happy about this and so the Doctor agreed that perhaps he would get better attention here in his own home.

I immediately told Mum that there was no way we would be going away as we were so concerned about my father! With that Mum asked us if we would stay with her over the weekend and thought it would be a good idea especially seeing dad so ill. Saturday was awful as Dad seemed to get worse, I really feared for his life so much! On the Sunday morning when we got up, I went to my father's room. Dad looked such a different person; he seemed to have taken on a better colour to his face and looked more his usual self. I asked him how he felt today and he said that he was 100% better. What a relief this was for all of us! He told us that he was going to get up, have a wash, shave and also that he'd have something to eat because he felt so hungry. This made all of us feel loads better ourselves and felt that at last he was on the mend.

Mum asked if Joanne and I might go to the supermarket and get some shopping, as she hadn't been able to get out since Dad had been ill. I said we would go to get some supplies for them, so off we went, including Lindsay. I think we'd probably been gone about an hour, but we'd also made a visit to Clenchwarton, this is about 6 miles away from mum and dad's, we had gone to visit some friends. We eventually got back to Middleton where they lived. I had just turned the corner into their cul-de-sac only to see an ambulance and a police car outside my parents' bungalow. Alarm bells rang in my mind and I told Joanne to sit and wait in the car with Lindsay.

As I walked up to the bungalow I was met at the door by my younger brother. He said to me that Dad had gone; of course I knew what this meant, he'd died! I just couldn't believe this, we had left him just over an hour ago looking so well and sprightly. Dad had suffered a massive heart attack which had been brought on by the emphysema. Of course this was a dreadful shock for everyone; it seemed so unreal, especially when I'd left him along with mother looking so much better than I'd seen him over the previous days. I believe at times we all think we're going to be around indefinitely, but then the reality kicks in; it's dreadful when things like this happen. Over the next few days arrangements were made for Dad's funeral, everything was put in order, as it should be done.

I will never ever forget my Dad as long as I live; he had been such a brilliant father to me. Over the years I've spent so many hours in hospitals, he was always there to make sure I was where I had to be, he had driven me miles, we had travelled on trains also to make sure that I attended my appointments at all of these places, and now he was gone! Even today when I have to make a trip on the train to in London I think of my Dad and how he would travel with me. It's a lovely memory, but I feel so sad that he's not there with me although having said this I still feel his presence there by my side.

My Mum, I love her so much! There will always be the memory of Mother that will go with me for the rest of my life, and that was when I about eighteen. I woke one morning to sense that there was something really different about my face, it felt so strange. It wasn't until I got up and went to the bathroom that I looked in the mirror to see my face. It had all blown up to twice it's normal size and my eye was protruding very badly. I was in such a terrible state, I think it must have been shock. I can see myself standing there now at the top of our stairs calling her to come up and look at me. She consoled me and insisted that I would be all right. The doctor was called in straightaway and it was found that I had chicken pox; this had badly affected my eye. I think it seems to be the case when something happens like this, when you have a fragility of some kind or other, it always goes to the weakest point. Within a few days things started to settle down, but this had made a terrible difference to my looks. However my mother was always there for me reassuring me, that everything would be absolutely fine.

Several weeks went by and I seemed to go into a state of depression. As you can imagine, my mother was desperately worried about me and already aware of what was happening. As the days passed, Mum had been talking to one of her friends, who said that she knew of a spiritualist healer. I feel that Mum thought that this might be the help I needed, as nothing else could be done for me in the medical sense at the time. I had already been having operations, but they just didn't seem to make much difference. The reason that Mother had come up with this idea was that her friend had once been suffering from what was called a withered hand. She had visited a spiritualist healer a few times, a man called Mr. Charles Laflin. She said that her hand had miraculously been cured, and so it was thought that this man might even be able to help me too.

An appointment was made for me to meet Charles, who lived in Ipswich. We would go to her friend's house; she lived in Brandon. It must have cost my mother absolutely loads of money to do this, because we were travelling from King's Lynn by taxi every time. I think we may have done this about four times over a few weeks, but this was my mother's caring way. She felt that it was worth giving it a try, as it might help me with my terrible eye condition, and especially as there was nothing to lose by doing this. It would be a miracle if something did happen anyway! I even went and stayed at her friend's house in Brandon for a few days so that I could travel with her on an odd occasion. Regrettably no miracle ever happened for me from going on these trips, but in my own mind I must admit, I did feel better about my condition. When you think about it, I suppose in a certain sort of way it did help me!

BROTHERLY LOVE

As you know, I have an elder and a younger brother by three and seven years respectively. Chris lives near to Watton in Norfolk and Adrian is fairly close to my own home in Heacham. People who have brothers and sisters themselves know that there will always be rivalry in one's younger years, and our lives were just like anybody else's. All three of us fought like cat and dog, but I believe this was merely a part of growing up, and as the saying goes 'Boys will be boys'. When I look back I know that I had been quite vindictive towards Adrian because we used to get into some rough and tumbles. Whenever I wasn't winning, the fight I would call Mum and tell her that he had hit me and that he had made me cry! Unfortunately poor old Adrian used to come off the worse for wear because my mother would then tell him off, saying that he should be very careful not to injure me because of my medical condition. We very often speak of this now but I do feel awful in what I did however, Adrian and I just laugh about how we were and what we did!

I do love both my brothers very dearly and feel that as we've grown older we've grown to love each other more strongly than ever before; it's always so good to be able to get together and talk of the events of our childhood. I must just state though that I don't spend half enough time with either of them, and feel rather bad about this, but I know that if ever I were in trouble in any way they would soon be there to stand by me through thick and thin.

Just as a matter of interest I would like to tell a little story regarding my incredible brothers and their wonderful ways. Since I've been writing this book I want just to mention that Joanne and I have struggled though our life because of having poor paid jobs. Managing our money has been quite difficult for many years and especially due to the fact that I've only been able to work a few hours a week because of my disability. A few days before my mother's eightieth birthday my brothers decided that we should celebrate this in style. Although I know my mother probably wouldn't want this to be common knowledge, she absolutely adores her horse racing! Chris and Adrian had arranged for a day out for some of the family to go to Newmarket races, unbeknown to Mother. We all met outside her house in a minibus and to her surprise she was taken to the races for the day! Now because of our financial situation I was rather concerned that we hadn't the money to enable us to take part on this memorable milestone in my mother's life.

Both Chris and Adrian took me to one side and told me that it was nothing to worry about and that it was all in order; they had paid for everything. I must admit I do have terrible feelings of guilt about this even now. Their answer to this was, "We're your brother's and that's what brothers do for each other in times of need." I was deeply moved by what they did for us on that day and want them to know what this meant to me. I know in my heart of hearts that they already know this anyway, but I must just say how much I love them both and would do exactly the same for them too should the opportunity arise.

Way back in the summer of 2015 both Joanne and I were invited over to Adrian's to stay for the weekend. Ady as we call him, suggested that we go for an evening out at his local pub, the Anvil at Congham. It's probably around about a 2 mile walk down country lanes from his house to the pub. We started off at his village local where we had a pint before we walked off to Congham. When we arrived at the Anvil, a live band was playing , the atmosphere was electric and we really got into the music, of course the drinks were flowing too!.Before we knew it the evening had gone by. Both Ady and I were fairly well tanked up, in fact we were both literally legless. Poor Joanne, I really don't know how she coped with two drunkards as we staggered our way home.

Both Ady and I fell in and out of the hedges as we gradually walked along. On one occasion I couldn't get up for laughing, it was so funny, and all the time Joanne was trying her hardest to keep us on the move, she was as sober as a Judge. Ady fell in the hedge once more and this time he lost his glasses, oh dear, it was so funny! Joanne has always been the sensible one, she had purchased a packet of crisps earlier in the evening. and had the sense to throw the packet down where Ady had fallen. We eventually got back to his house where we all went off to bed.

The next morning when we got up, we were both suffering from the side effects of over doing the drink the previous night. Ady then mentioned that not only had he lost his glasses but had fallen on his mobile phone and broken the screen. However, on a positive note, he'd walked his dog earlier that morning, down the lanes where we'd had our adventurous ramble home. He found his glasses a few feet from where Joanne had thrown her packet of crisps down. What a great night, what a brilliant laugh. I know it may sound as if it was a bit of a mad night out, but we just had the biggest and best night of our lives. I love him to bits, what a brother!

GRANDFATHER & GRANDMOTHER

My grandparents on both sides of the family played a major part in my life, especially Ted and Laura Sutton. On one of my visits to see them down at Heath Farm, I was sitting on the back of Mother's new bicycle that Grandad had bought for her. I can see myself now, it's such a vivid picture of me riding on the back the bike, sitting in this square black seat on a very bumpy singled tracked dirt road. This particular morning was rather frosty and my mother was making her usual trip to see Grandmother and Grandfather from the village of Thompson into the battle area.

The track had large potholes that had filled with water, and this of course had frozen over. The sound of the crack of the ice as we rode along sounded so good. Can you imagine how cold this must have been on a bicycle? My Mum got frostbite in her fingers, as she had no gloves. I was always dressed for the weather; a little woollen vest was always worn and warm thick clothing was a real necessity on those cold days. When we used to arrive at the farmhouse Grandfather's big old white geese would be honking and I was always so frightened by them. I was such a little lad, only as tall as they were! In latter years, while living at Stow Bedon, Grandfather kept Canada geese and these were even worse. The noise that they kicked up when anybody came by was dreadful, and I expect this was one of the reasons that he had them, in case there were strangers about near his property. "They won't hurt you" Grandfather always said, but I never gave them a chance to get near me. I would rush indoors to get out of the way, but not only that I was looking forward to see my dear Grandmother.

Grandfather was very particular about appearance of the farmhouses at Heath Farm, also at Stow Bedon; the upper parts of the buildings where painted in a product called Snowcem and the cobbled brickwork round the bottom of the farmhouse was coated in thick black shiny paint, it may well even have been a kind of tar. I remember how this reflected the sunlight when it was bright and sunny. There was a type of courtyard at Heath Farm with stables on the outer walls for the cattle and other livestock. The cattle could be left inside this courtyard during bad weather. My grandfather always loved this place, although it could be so desolate in the winter. In latter years he told me that he wished he had never moved away from there.

We used to visit both the Sutton and Bird grandparents every other week in turn; these visits were mostly done on bicycles and was to be so until my father got his first car. My grandmother had brought up a large family, four boys and four girls, and food for her offspring was one of the most important tasks along with the other work that had to be done on the farm. Grandmother was such a marvelous cook and her house was always full of family and friends. Anybody could turn up to see them and there would always be enough food to go round. Her cooking was always wholesome and everyone enjoyed going to visit them especially for this fantastic cuisine.

How she ever managed to cope with all of this wonderful cooking I don't know, she always seemed to take it in her stride, but I expect that it was the fact that she had brought up all of these children. She had to provide for them, whatever the circumstances. Quite often several of the family members would be asked to go to dinner at Stow Bedon; it was nothing unusual for there to be 15 or more for Sunday dinner and tea at the farmhouse. The food would be served up in two rooms as we couldn't all get round one table. There would be perhaps Elliott, Dora, Glendy, Paul, Jayne, Elizabeth, Uncle Tom and Aunt Jessie, my mother and father, Chris, Adrian, myself and of course Grandmother and Grandfather. The food would be so tasty! One other leading factor regarding this was that she had been in service in her earlier years and had cooked for big families.

I once remember her telling me the story about having helped prepare a meal for the ill-fated Tsar and Tsarina of Russia. I'm not quite certain if this was a true story or where this took place, but she had worked for a Major Birkbeck at Stratton Strawless Hall. This may well have been a place that they could have visited if they came to England but I feel this is one of those stories like we all tell at times. It may well have been some other big, well known family of that era that visited the hall. But, as you can see, her skills to deal with all sizes of family and all sorts of people were well in hand, and she never seemed to get stressed at all.

Grandmother was always busy in the kitchen; her oven always seemed to be full of food cooking, she very often had a large pot sitting on the top and the smells coming from this would be wonderful. There was one particular holiday when I had been staying there with them and she said that she had cooked something special just for me. I asked her what it was going to be; she said that I was to try it first. She put a plate on the table before me with the meat and vegetables and I began to eat. It was wonderful, I had never tasted such a flavour before. I ate the lot and asked her what I had eaten, but I was a bit shocked when she said I had just consumed a moorhen. Had I known, I don't think I would have even tried it, but I can assure you it was so tasty!

I spent many happy hours with my grandparents, even up until my early teens, and this was mostly at Stow Bedon, where they had their smallholding. This little piece of land had a few acres where he would keep a few livestock. It also had an orchard with apple and plum trees. When school holidays came round, I looked forward to having at least one week staying with them on the farm; I loved being there with both of them. Grandmother would get me helping when she did the baking, or at least I thought I was helping anyway. A bit of pastry that had been left over especially for me was always great fun, making little men with faces made from currants. They never really turned out very well, but I used to eat them all the same. Grandmother also used to make her own butter from the milk that Grandad had taken from the cows earlier in the day. She had this small glass milk churn, and she would let me help her to make the butter. When the butter had been formed after churning, I would use wooden butter pats to shape it into an oblong ready for use in the kitchen. I would then perhaps go out with Grandad to feed the chickens, geese and animals; there was also an old machine in the shed, this had a large hopper that he would fill up with sugar beet or mangolds. You then turned the handle and this would slice them up and then used to feed the cattle. When I got big enough to be able to stand on a box, he would let me have a go. This was great fun.

As the years went by, my affection for my grandparents grew even stronger. They were both wonderful people whom I dearly loved. One particular day while staying at Stow Bedon, I just happened to be looking for Grandad but couldn't find him, so I asked Grandmother where he might be. She said that he could be in the barn or in the sheds. I went to look, and there he was. He must have just slaughtered a sheep, as it was hung up on the lintel of the doorway. A wheelbarrow was placed underneath the sheep and he had just slit its belly, as all the intestines came out and fell into the barrow. I stood there watching him, fascinated by what he was doing, I don't suppose it even bothered me seeing him do this, but when I think about it now, I can't imagine I would be able to bear it these days. Farming and butchery had been my grandfather's trade, and his father's before him, so this was just natural to him.

I do have an exceptionally wonderful memory of my grandfather, which has stayed with me all of my life. Grandmother used to take him to Bury St. Edmunds to the cattle market once a week. One holiday time that I was there with them I went to Bury too. Grandad had never driven a car, but in his earlier years he went by horse and cart. Granny Sutton, as all her grandchildren called her, drove a grey Austin A40 van, and we went off to Bury market on this particular Wednesday. "Stop the car, Laura!" he said. "Why

what's the matter" she said. "I want to cut the boy a stick."
Grandfather always walked round the market with a stick, as
did all the other farmers and dealers. This was used when
looking at the livestock. He would use this to make the cattle,
sheep and pigs move around the pens to look to see what
sort of shape the animals were in before he made a bid for
them. He wanted me to have a stick so that I could learn to do
the same as he did.

     While Grandfather was having a deal, Grandmother
and I would very often go round the market place to buy the
food for the week. Bury St. Edmunds was quite a busy,
bustling town and the wonderful atmosphere is hard to
comprehend. When we got back from shopping we would
meet him in the Market Tavern, where he would buy me a
glass of lemonade. This was a very special treat for me, as my
parents didn't have much money in those days and I felt
great seeing my grandfather with all of his fellow farmer
friends. I held him in such great esteem and loved him so
dearly; my trips with my grandparents will always be in my
memories.

     Grandfather and Granny Bird lived at Great Hockham.
Visits to them would usually mean a bike ride from
Thompson to Hockham. The bicycles would come out again,
this was the main mode of transport from one village to
another, and it was not at all unusual to cycle four or five
miles and think nothing of it. I will always look back on these
trips as out of the ordinary days, because we would all get
dressed up in our best clothes. To think we'd only be being
going out on bicycles (me on the back in a seat on my

mother's bike, and Adrian on the back of Dad's along with Chris on his little Raleigh hand-me-down) and yet we'd be so excited by this trip to see our grandparents! I think it's the fact that my parents didn't have much money, and a visit like this was considered a special treat!

There's yet another memory that comes to mind, it's that Dad had always used Brylcream on his hair; and this was no exception for me either. I expect you'll laugh when I say that my Dad would groom my hair and put it into what we would call a quiff. I suppose you could call it some sort of a hairstyle of the sixties. I wouldn't be happy unless he'd done this right every time, because I know I'd look in the mirror to admire this great hairstyle.

On nearly every trip to see Grandfather Bird, Adrian and I would be asked if we would like one of the tools from this large wooden chest that was kept in the conservatory. He would open up the chest and say, "You can have one thing out of there each." We would then pick something that would take our fancy. I still have a couple of odd things that we were given to me all those years ago, one them being a brace and bit although the handles are full of woodworm now.

Granny Bird loved her TV. This poor old lady had been an invalid since her early 50's, and I believe she'd had a stroke. Grandfather had cared for and looked after her in all of those years, but I think she had enjoyed her life none the less for this. I can just see her now, sitting in her Lloyd Loom chair waiting patiently for her favourite programme to come on, this being "Songs of Praise". She would be singing away to all the hymns, her favourite being "The Old Rugged Cross." When this was over the following programme was usually 'Dr Finlay's Casebook;' this was the most boring part of our trip and couldn't wait for Mum and Dad to say we had to make a move. I know that my brothers and I would be getting itchy feet and wanting to get ourselves back home again.

In 1970, Grandmother died. She had lived a long life regardless of her disability, and was into her 86th year. Sadly, three years later Grandfather died and was of the same age. He had always liked his beer, and having been to the Eagle pub, he had taken a fall on his way home. Workmen had been doing some repair work in the street, and he had stumbled over where the ground had been dug up. In those days sadly signs were not used to warn people of the digging, and obviously he had misjudged his footing. I expect the beer hadn't helped either. He was taken to the doctor's, and they found that he had broken his hip. Within a few weeks of this happening he died.

MOVING HOUSE

We moved from Well Corner into another house further down the village. This was right next door to the village hall and was part of the blacksmith's cottage; we were in the middle, but next door to the Nunn family. Mr & Mrs. Walter Nunn and their son Arthur were really lovely people. I think Arthur must have been in his late fifties; this seemed to me like being an old man. I was talking to the son one day and called him by his first name. My mother happened to be outside and heard me call him Arthur; I was severely reprimanded for this and told that I must respect my elders. From that time on he was called Mr. Nunn.

Walter had been the village blacksmith up until his retirement and was a lovely old boy. Unbeknown to him, behind his back we called him Skinny Nunn. He was always busy in the village with his scythe; this old man cut all of the grass verges immaculately in the near vicinity of his house. On Mondays Mrs. Nunn would do her washing outside in an old galvanised wash tub full of hot water. She then used a zinc scrubbing board to rub the clothes on to remove the dirt, and then perhaps use a Dolly. This looked like a three-legged stool on an upright handle that was used to agitate the water.

Our small kitchen, or scullery as we knew it, had an old copper tub where mother would do her weekly washing. There was a small stove below, and this would be lit to get the water as hot as possible, I remember her using a little blue bag that she would put into the water to help bring the whites up even whiter! I know for a fact that this little bag was often used during the latter part of the season too, when wasps were around. If you got stung, this little bag would be dampened and pressed onto the area of the puncture wound that was hurting, this would supposedly take away the pain. I don't know if this actually worked or not, but I would imagine it was one of those "old wives tales" a way of trying to ease the soreness.

After the washing had been done, Mother would rinse this all in fresh water and it would then be put through the wringer. This was an item that would get most of the water out of the washing. It had two rubber rollers mounted on top of each other that could be adjusted to the thickness of the material you'd been washing, and you'd then pass the washing through. It had a handle on the side that you would turn, and as the items passed through the water would be expelled into a small tin bath or bucket below. You might well think that all of this was very old fashioned, but we had more modern ways than that of our neighbour next door as she had been using the older methods for washing her clothes and linen. Things have changed so much such since the early sixties and may I hasten to add not for the better!

The toilets at this house were just outside the back of the building; this was just a little wooden shed. It was so awful to have to go outside in the dark to go to the toilet. The bench was made from a long piece wood, which had been carved to form a seat, but in this case there was one hole for the adults and a smaller hole for the children, and these were side by side. How convenient, so to speak. Toilet paper was a luxury and we hardly ever had any. Most of the time we had to use cut-up squares of newspaper, which was hung up on a bit of string that had been threaded through all the cut pieces of paper. What a smell! It was dreadful, I can even picture it now how it used to be, we were so poor.

About once a month, or whenever the buckets were full, poor Dad would have to dig a big hole down the bottom of the garden to empty them. This must have been such an awful task for him to have to do. I never ever remember my father complaining; this was a job that had to be done, whatever. We were always told to go and play while Dad did this but I remember watching! Am I glad I never had to do this, but it was just the way of life. At night-time we had guzunders as they were called. For those of you who don't know the term, they were china toilet pots that were placed underneath the bedstead, which you could use during the night-time should you need to have a wee. My mother would empty these the next morning and they would smell awful too. Today the kids don't know half of what went on. I know that it has been said many times before by our elders, and even ourselves that the young people of today don't really know how well off they are, as I am sure they would squirm at the thought of having to do the things we did in those days. Ah! Those were the days!

My elder brother and I shared a bed in this little cottage, and it was like living in the Arctic in the winter. We had masses of blankets on the beds, and sometimes even old overcoats, these were so heavy in order to keep ourselves warm from the winter chill. We only had the wooden floorboards to walk on, apart from the small rugs that were placed beside the bed. These were made up from small cut-off pieces of coloured rag, but I suppose it saved our feet from getting splinters when we got out of bed. The wintertime always seemed really cold, hard frosts were nothing unusual. When we got up in the mornings we'd go to the window to draw the curtains. You could see the steam from our breath as we exhaled, it was that cold! We would try to rub a small hole on the ice that had formed on the window pane, but the ice would be far too thick, it was obviously thicker on the outside too. We would hurriedly get dressed in the hope that Mother had perhaps made a fire downstairs in the kitchen, so that we could get warmed through once again. Downstairs the floors were covered with linoleum, including the sitting room, but this was always kept so clean. I can remember my mother scrubbing the floors on her hands and knees to keep our little house spotless.

Bath-time was quite an event in our house. We had an old galvanised bathtub that hung up on the wall outside our back door; this was brought into the house about twice a week and would be put in front of the open fire. The saucepans would be put on the cooker and also on a small paraffin stove, to heat up some water for a bath as we had no immersion heater in those days. We would each take turns in using the water. Obviously the last person to have a bath would have the dirtiest water, though we never came to any harm in doing this. There is a memory that I have regarding the bathtub, it was one particular Saturday; we sat eating our dinner and all of a sudden there was such a bang, we thought that the bath had fallen off the wall. We all went rushing out to see why it had fallen off. This wasn't the case. To our dismay there had been a car accident on the crossroads just outside our house. An elderly gentleman had misjudged the speed of another car coming down the main road; he had gone across the junction and had smashed into the oncoming car. My parents got the old gentleman out and he was badly shaken. An ambulance was called and he was taken off to hospital, where he made a full recovery.

School Days

As the years went by I mixed with all the kids in the village, but eventually it was time for me to go to the local school. My family and friends never questioned about the fact that I was disabled and had a severe facial disfigurement; everybody in the village whom I grew up with knew me, and my disfigurement was never ever spoken about. As far as they were concerned I was normal, just like everyone else, I was the same and nobody treated me any differently.

The very first day that I went to primary school, my mother and I walked from our house along with the old school-mistress. I think her name was Mrs Platford. She was a tall, plump lady but she was such a happy-go-lucky person, I immediately fell in love with her because she was so kind. It was such a wonderful day in my life, but I just couldn't understand why some of the children were crying as their mothers left them. I thought, what were all these tears for? I suppose it had been the fact that I had always been willing to stay with anybody as a small child growing up, and there was no fear of my being left with someone else. The classes were quite small, and I think that there were probably only fifteen of us. The lessons were conducted using a chalkboard on an easel, and each child had a small individual chalkboard too. There was so much to do at the school, every day was exciting, but if you got tired they had small fold-up beds that you could go and lie down on.

The first year went by, and then in the following year my cousin Paul started school. Paul was like another brother to me and we were inseparable. We used play games in the schoolyard at break times. I remember on one occasion we were playing some kind of game where you had to run after each other; once you had caught somebody; you had to run holding each other's hand to catch the next person. We were trying to catch someone and Paul pulled me over onto the ground accidentally. I grazed my knee and cried. One of the other children thought that Paul had deliberately hurt me and reported this to the headmistress. We were taken in and the teacher tore him off a strip or two and asked him what he had done to me, I said that he hadn't hurt me, it was someone else; I didn't want him to get wrong. I would have gone through hell and high water not to see him being told off by the schoolteacher for this; he was and still is one of my favourite cousins.

At the weekend I used to go and play with my mates. I remember one particular day we all went up to the school. We really shouldn't have been there really as it was out of bounds at the week-ends. But as children we didn't take much notice of this. On this particular week-end there were about two or three of us and we were running around the school playground, and then we decided to play hide-and-seek or something similar. The other boys went and hid and I tried looking for them. They were nowhere to be seen. I climbed up onto the boys' toilet block because there was a coal heap, this was quite high, this enabled me to get up onto the wall where I could get a better view. As you probably already know, in days gone by places like school toilets were of course outside and just open to the elements.

Just across the way from the school was the Belham's house. On this particular day that we'd been playing in the schoolyard, a member of the family must have been ill as Dr. Shanks arrived in his car. When he came back out of the house, I thought I would play a bit of a trick on him. I acted as if I was dead on top of this toilet block. He shouted across to me to see if I was OK. I lay there for quite a few moments and then the Doctor came walking across the schoolyard to check to see if I was all right. I got up off the toilet block and ran away. I don't know if he told my mother and father, but at the time I thought it was quite funny. However, looking back I now realise what I had done. What a silly boy and what stupid tricks. By the way, I never did find my mates, they must have gone home.

Mrs. Seaman was the head teacher; she was quite a nice woman. One particular term she had a visitor who had come over from Arizona in the United States. Several of us went on an organised trip to London from the school and he came along with us too. This was my first visit to the big city. I know that we went to visit Madame Tussauds and we had to go on the tube. This American chap got his fingers trapped in the sliding doors of the tube train. I had never been on a trip or anything like this before, this was a brilliant adventure for a little country boy. I sometimes wonder how the teachers managed to keep us all under control; anyway, we all got back home safely. A few years went by, and Mrs Seaman retired, we then had a stand-in head teacher called Mr. Poulton. He seemed to be quite a likeable chap, but didn't stay there too long.

In due course, a permanent head teachor arrived, her name was Mrs. Newton. I totally adored her; she was so kind to us all. Each Easter-time she would buy us all an small Easter egg. Another thing that I really loved about her was the art lessons that she gave, she taught me so much about drawing and painting, she always seemed to be so interested in all that we did.

Two or three times each year, the school inspector turned up; we all feared him. He was over six foot tall, dark haired and a very sombre-looking man; he seemed like a giant and towered above us all. He was there to check up that all the kids were coming to school. I don't know why I should have been frightened by him, as I never really had much time off from school, that is apart from my hospital visits. These were allowed but there were certain children who always seemed to be away school every time, he was there to see why. We would sit there in the classroom while he stood chatting to the teacher, and we would glance at him. Occasionally he would realise that we were looking and he would give a hard stare back; this frightened us even more.

As we moved up into the higher class, we sat at double desks. These were tables that had inkwells and pencil ridges; I can never ever recall using a ballpoint pen at this first school, well at least not until we went to the secondary modern. We used our pencils for writing in work books once we were in the senior classroom, a pencil sharpener was fixed on the school window-sill and was a good excuse to get up and go away from our desk for a minute or two so that we could have a break from a lesson that was perhaps getting a bit boring. The teacher eventually realised what we were up to and this little excursion was soon stopped!

In the school there were only two classrooms, one for the juniors and one for the seniors. These were rather large airy rooms, by that I mean, with tall ceilings. The heating in both rooms was right out of the Ark; they had this big round black burner in the middle of the room with a little door with glass windows that could be opened for coal to be thrown in with a shovel. There was a long, tall chimney that reached to the ceiling and a large fireguard that surrounded fireplace; this was there to stop any of the children getting burnt.

Any time between the late spring term and up until summer break we would have at least one sports day when Philip Newton, our teacher's husband, would come and mark out the field with white washed lines for the big occasion. This day consisted of egg and spoon races, sack races and much more. Our mothers would be there to watch, and from what I remember, it always seemed to be on hot sunny days.

It was while at this school that I was to suffer an accident to my eye, which really made my condition much worse than it already was. We were playing rounders in the school playground one dinnertime when the teacher came out to ring the bell for us to go back into class. The young chap who had the rounders bat in his hand had thrown it over his shoulder, and I just happened to be in the wrong place at the wrong time. The bat hit me straight in my eye. They took me inside and I recollect sitting in the classroom crying. It wasn't really for the fact that it hurt badly, but it was that I was so anxious that my mother would go mad at me over this terrible accident. In those days there didn't seem to be the care regarding first aid, and my teacher didn't even do anything to help with the accident that had occurred. I don't think she realised the seriousness of what had happened.

I got home after school and my mother was so shocked; this had caused terrible irreparable harm to my eye. They rushed me to my doctor, but the damage had already taken place and nothing could be done to help me. The swelling in and around my eye took several weeks to get back to some sort of normality. From that day on I was never ever allowed to play games and sport of any type again and I really felt cheated by this, as I had always enjoyed taking part in all these events.

WORKING PARENTS

Father had worked at numerous jobs for other people over a period of time, but eventually found employment working for another farmer at Thompson. Geoff Quadling was a dealer in Aylesbury ducklings and my father helped throughout the year to rear, kill and pluck the ducklings ready for Christmas. Dad also had another string to his bow, and that was as a lorry driver for Geoff.

After Dad started at Qualding's farm, we moved from our house that was rented to a property that belonged to Geoff. Apparently he bought the house so that my parents could live there. My father used to regularly do the accounts for Geoff and for doing this there would be no charge for living in the house and so it was rent-free. Dad always worked Saturday mornings and came home around dinnertime. I can remember that every Saturday, after we had eaten our dinner, Chris my elder brother and I would be kicking each other's feet under the table, this argument was over who was going to ask Dad for some pocket money (sixpence if we were lucky). We used to hate to ask, as it was very difficult in those days to cope on the wages that he brought home. Pocket money was not always possible; however there was another way that we would get ourselves some money. There was an old pit in our village that people would use as a rubbish dump, and to supplement the sixpence assuming we got it, we would go to the pit as people used to throw their odd bits of household waste down there. If you were lucky, sometimes you could find their empty beer and ginger beer bottles that had been chucked away into it.

We would collect the best ones that we could find and take them home to wash. We would then take back to The Chequers, this was the village pub, we'd give them to Mr Blake. Hopefully we would get penny on each bottle for returning them. This was quite productive for a few weeks, but then the supply of bottles eventually came to an end.

If Dad had any extra money, which was a rare occasion, we would cycle to the Regal Cinema at Watton. I would be on the seat at the back of Mothers' bike and Chris and Dad would go on their bikes. There were cycle sheds at the cinema, and the majority of people who came here would be on their bicycles as car ownership was quite rare in those days. Nobody ever had locks on their bikes; thieving was something that rarely ever happened. I can even recall Mum and Dad leaving the house unlocked most of the time; days like this have gone forever. Trust was such a wonderful thing in those days.

As time went by I wanted to learn to ride my brother's old bike. Initially my brother tried to help me to learn by holding onto the seat, and he would run behind me while I steered and peddled away. I soon got the hang of it after a few falls; however, I do remember one particular day having learned to ride, that I was coming back from the top end of the village, a wasp had gone down the front of my tee shirt. I had this feeling of something crawling down inside my clothes, I slapped my chest only to be stung by the wasp, then into the bargain I fell off my bike straight into a bunch of stinging nettles. That was not one of my better days.

The bike was one of the best things that ever happened to me. My dear old Grandmother actually had a win on the football pools and bought me a brand spanking new bike, this was really wonderful after having had the old hand me down from my brother. We used to go out cycling for miles and miles and there never seemed to be any worries about strangers taking you away, it was something that never heard of in those days. The sixties were such a wonderful times to be a child and we were so care free!

My mother also contributed to bringing money into the house. During the spring she would get up very early in the mornings (about 4:30am) to go off chopping out sugar beet. This was a backbreaking job but it had to be done, in order to earn some money to survive. Mother would come back home around 7:00am to let Dad go off to work and then Mum would get us off to school. She would then go back again to chopping out the beet, she would then be home for us when we left off school. Mother worked on the land in lots of other ways too. She would go carrot pulling and topping, onion peeling, bean picking and several various other jobs throughout the year, it had been an extremely hard life for my parents, but we all survived.

Norris's, the village shop, was just a few doors away from us. Betty Norris owned the shop along with her husband, used to help us out by letting mother have her groceries all the week without paying; anything that Mother wanted from this shop used to go into a little red book. At the end of the week on father's payday, Mother would go see Betty and settle up her bill. I'm almost certain that if Betty hadn't helped in this way we would have struggled to have enough food to last through the week. Betty never queried doing this for my mother, because there was so much trust in everyone in those days. Unfortunately this doesn't happen today, and I'm sure you can understand why!

Every six weeks or so we would walk down to Bob Carter's. Bob was the village hairdresser; he had a shed down at the bottom end of his garden, with just had an ordinary old wooden household chair to sit on while your hair was being cut. His hairdressing tools were right out of the Ark. In those days there was no electricity down in his garden shed, he just used a pair of hand clippers. They were OK but if you struck unlucky and it was the time when they needed oiling and sharpening, you would more than likely to get a nip in the neck. It would cost sixpence to have the haircut and Bob would always ask how you wanted your hair done today. It didn't matter what you asked for, it would always be the same! It was just like having a bowl put over your head and the hair would be cut all around it. Poor old Bob, he was such a lovely old boy. Of course there was yet another danger in having your haircut by Bob, he used to smoke his cigarette while cutting your hair, the ash would sometimes drop off and go down the back of your neck. He never said a word, but you can imagine what it would be like with a hot ember falling down the back of your neck and into the bargain he'd just nicked your skin with his clippers too! What a painful experience!

Chris and I went to church every other week to attend Sunday school. This was about a mile down the village towards Stow Bedon. Most of the village children did this, and Canon King took the services. This dear old gentleman married my mother and father in the June of 1949, and even prepared me for my confirmation at the village church in Griston a few years later.

High Days & Holidays

During the summer holidays we would go along with Mother wherever she worked on the land, me sitting on the back of her bike, and my brother Chris would ride alongside her on his. Mother used to take a pack-up and flask of tea with her, and we would all sit at the headland at dinner times enjoying this. This was another great adventure for us children; we only had a few little Dinky toys to play with in the dirt but we were always contented by all of this. We were never fed up, so to speak, as there was always lots to see and do even if we were out for most of the day.

There were always exciting days to look forward to, and on one particular day that I remember, the sun was shining and it was so hot. We all went off to a field just outside the village where my uncle, was harvesting the barley. On this particular field was an old pond where the water was so clear and inviting. Two cousins and I got into the water and we were paddling, when my aunt appeared on the scene to tell us all off for being in there. We couldn't understand what we were doing wrong, we were having such a lovely time in this cool clear water. Looking back now I realise how frightening this must have been for her, it was the thought of us being drowned. When you're young you see no fear, and playing in a pond in the hot weather seemed like a great idea!

We would also spend time with Dad when we were on holiday from school, as we used to go with him in Geoff's lorry to Methwold to pick up the ducklings from a chap who used to rear them in big sheds. We would help them load these ducklings into their crates ready to travel back to Thompson. Very often we would be given an odd duckling to hand-rear in our own garden as we absolutely adored our animals.

Pets had always played an important part in our lives, especially dogs. When I was a little lad, and even up to the time when I left home to get married, we always had a dog. The first dog that my mother and father had was a German Shepherd. Her name was Sheila; she was such a lovely dog, especially with the children. Sheila had lived up until she was ten or eleven but was taken ill, and Dad had to take her to the vets'. She had to be put to sleep. My poor Mum cried and cried, as it had been just like losing one of the family.

We then had a little Jack Russell called Pepi; he could be a vicious little dog sometimes. Brother Chris and I would walk him round the village, and one day while on one of these walks we went by Mrs Strowger's house. They had a big black Labrador-type dog. It came running out from their yard and poor Chris had Peppy on the lead. The black dog was trying to attack the Jack Russell. The next thing I knew was that Chris was swinging the dog round and round by his lead to try to prevent the Labrador biting him. Poor little Peppy soaring through the air, I think he must have gone dizzy, but the owner came out and took the big dog away. Peppy was OK, but what a fright for us and also for the little Jack Russell; I think he must have thought he was having flying lessons! You couldn't trust him with anyone, not even with my parents, and he ruled the roost, as you would say. He was kept outside during the day on a chain that was tethered to an old open beer barrel; this was open at one end so that he could get inside if it rained. His bedding was inside the barrel, so at least he could keep warm and dry. He was then brought back in at nighttimes when we had gone to bed. Another reason for him being kept out there was because of his aggressiveness towards people if they came to the house. We always had a fear that he might bite someone one day.

A few years went by and he did actually bite some little lad. As you can imagine, my parents were so worried by what had happened and decided that they couldn't keep him any longer. One of my uncles used to go to some big hall out in the country, there he knew a person who kept hounds that were used for hunting foxes, and so he was given away to them. From time to time we would ask my uncle about him. He told us that he lived in great style along with all the other hunt dogs and this carried on until his dying day. What a happy conclusion for this aggressive little dog, it could have been a very different story for him as he may have finished up being put to sleep. Of course both Chris and I were upset to see this little dog go from our home, but at least we realised that it was the right thing to do. I'm sure that I must have cried about this happening, but I always had mates who had dogs and cats that I could make a fuss of.

Over the summer holidays I would spend time with my friends, one being Jamie Roberts. Jamie was my best mate and we were pretty inseparable. We loved to play cowboys and Indians. We had all the gear, cowboys and Red Indian suits, guns and hats and we made bows and arrows from the local wood, which was near to our home. Another favourite home-made toy was a catapult which was made from a y-shaped piece of wood which we would cut from a branch off a tree. We would then use a piece of knicker elastic for the launcher; this was great fun! We would also go scrumping for apples in the autumn. The crab-apples were great for putting on the ends of a long stick that was cut from out of the hedge, and this was then used to throw them at a fantastic distance. Life was great and every day was another voyage of discovery.

In our village every year they had a fete, it was usually during the school holidays, and this caused a great amount of stimulation. They would have had all the old kinds of stalls set up like, throwing a Ping Pong Ball into a Fish Bowl for a prize, Hit the Rat, this was a long piece pipe of some kind, and the rat would be a long sock that was stuffed with material to make it hard. The rat was dropped through the pipe and you had to hit it with a stick before it fell out at the very bottom. There were several other games like Hoopla, Lucky Dip, Bowling For The Pig, The Greasy Pole and of course there would be lots of food, drinks and ice-cream from the Dairyland van and many more other things to do.

My father was given an old car by his boss. I think it was an Austin Seven; it had spoked wheels and running boards. The front window was on hinges and you could open it outwards for ventilation during the summer. The seats of this were upholstered in leather and it was a lovely little old car. We sometimes went to Swaffham in this little car; this little market town has always been very dear to my heart as I have fond memories of going there. There was a small livestock market at the back of the Greyhound pub, and they would sell anything from pigs, goats and sheep to fowl. There were stalls surrounding the market square, and these ranged from clothing, household, butcher's, greengrocer's, plants and much more besides, people came from all over to visit this quaint little town.

A seaside trip was always looked forward to and one of our favourite haunts was Wells-next-the-Sea. Wells is a very small town on the northwest Norfolk coastline with a beautiful little harbour or quay. You will very often find the shellfish boats with their cargo, which would be mainly cockles, whelks and shrimps, uploading onto the harbour. You will also see several other small cruising boats and yachts that come up from the sea for mooring, especially during the summer months.

Our main reason for going to Wells was for some cockling. This was an annual event and during the summer holidays we would go with all our families, these included uncles, aunts & cousins including Laura, my grandmother who thoroughly enjoyed this trip to this lovely little town. You can drive up to the point which is not too far from the lifeboat house and park the cars. We would then make our way up over the high sand-bank via wooden steps. I believe these banks had been built up after the great floods of 1953, so it was quite a long trek upwards with all our gear to get to the beach.

On the left hand-side as you went down the steps were rows of beautifully painted beach huts, and in those days the people who came to this wonderful little beach filled these huts and the seashore to capacity. We would perhaps have a picnic when we got there. My cousins and I would play in and around the water, then it was decided that we would go off cockling. A chap would come up with his rowing boat and everybody would get on with his or her buckets, sacks and small hand rakes, he would take you across to the mudflats where you could go after the cockles. After raking and scraping we would fill our buckets with cockles, and these were taken all the way home to Thompson where Mum would boil them up on the stove. There's nothing like hot cockles! This was a real family day out, and a treat that we all looked forward to doing perhaps two or three times during the summer months.

We all looked forward to Christmas, and as children my elder brother and I would buy our parents a small present, but the first thing we had to do though was to ask for the money from Mother or Father to buy them as we hadn't got any. It seems funny now when I look back; we just didn't have money at all in those days, and it must have been a bit of a strain on my parents to be asked for the cash to buy them their gifts. You will probably laugh when I tell you that they both received the same thing every year. Dad would get a replacement stick of shaving soap and mum would have a tin of talcum power. People today don't realise how hard-up everybody was!

Our Christmas presents would consist of a main gift that Mother would buy from someone's club book, and then we would get an orange, an apple, a banana, some sweets, a chocolate box selection and probably a small net of golden foil-wrapped chocolate coins. If only children of today would realise how lucky they are now although having said this I think we were all very contented. There was, however, one year where we were exceptionally lucky. Dad's boss had a brother-in-law called Harry who gave us each a cane fishing rod. We couldn't believe it; it was as if we'd been given everything you could have wished for and even more, what wonderful Christmas presents these were.

The Waggon

The years went by and my parents managed to save some money, they started buying and rearing pigs. With the money that they had saved and with the help of Geoff Quadling the farmer, they managed to take over a tenancy of a public house in the adjoining village of Griston. This would be the place where I would encounter people whom I had never met before, these people would be seeing someone who had different facial features, and I wasn't too sure of how they would react to me. The name of the pub was, The Waggon and Horses, a lovely little old 18th century inn with lots of character.

R.A.F. Watton was just a stone's throw from Griston and Mum and Dad took over the Waggon and Horses. At that particular time, the Fleet Air Arm were stationed there. Quite a few of the R.A.F. personnel would come over to the pub when they had finished their working shift just to enjoy a pint or two and a good old chat. A strong and reliable trade was built up over the years with these people along with our local village customers. The R.A.F. boys and W.A.F. girls would use the pub for their parties. When they did, this they would start off by doing a collection for money in a bucket amongst themselves; this money would be used during the evening. Initially, they'd use up all of their paper money first, and then when this had gone, they'd start on their small change until their money in the bucket was used up. One particular evening a party was going on in the end bar and I walked down to see what all the noise was about. There, standing on one of the tables was a half-naked R.A.F. chap being sung to by his fellow comrades, the song, I vaguely remember, was called 'Zulu Warrior'. As the song went along more clothes came off, and the R.A.F. and W.A.F.'s were enjoying themselves. The next thing I knew, Dad sent me packing. I can just guess what happened next anyway, and I think the W.A.F.'s seemed to be enjoying this, were just as bad as the men!

Sadly one year there was a terrible accident at the station. I think that it may have been in 1966, but I'm not too sure of the exact date. My mother recollects that she was standing in the kitchen ironing; she heard such a loud bang. The next thing was that she looked out across the airfield to see flames, and black smoke that was billowing into the sky. I believe that tragically, two of the air crew were killed. A few days later after this accident I happened to be walking along one of the little roads not far from the accident site, I had picked up something metallic off of the road and took it home to show my Mum. She was really angry with me and said that I was to throw it away; she thought that it could have been something that had been blown off of the airplane as it exploded, it may well have been dangerous in some way, and feared that this could have hurt me. I threw it back into a ditch somewhere along the road.

Our pub was right opposite the St. Peter and St. Paul's church. One particular year this church was in desperate need of some new bell ropes, as the old ones were getting worn. An idea had been thought up that the locals of the community could go round collecting all of the old used newspapers from the village people, these would then be taken to the local scrap merchant who could recycle them for money. Everybody rallied round for months, especially the children; the local farmer lent us a hand-cart which could be used to collect these from each house. Enough money was raised and the new bell ropes were bought and hung. I believe Charles Banham may have done this; Charles was a churchwarden and also bell-ringer for Caston, in the next village, but he also rang for Griston too.

It was decided that because the village had bought the new ropes, some of the older children would be taught how to ring the bells, and I was going to be one of those kids. Because of my shortness I had to stand on a box and also a church pouffe; this then enabled me to be high enough to ring the bells. There was however one problem, before you could ring a bell, it had to be brought down into the ringing position. Once this is done, you're able to ring the bell. At the end of the session it had to be put up again into the resting position, and this was something more than I could ever have handled. It took quite a bit of strength to do this, so unfortunately due to my height and weight this was impossibility for me so one of the others would do it. You've probably seen something like this in comedy sketches, just imagine, me flying up into the air holding on to that rope! Within a few weeks of us starting this new hobby the local newspaper group caught wind of the story, they came to take photos, and they ran an article of how the church got its ropes and of how the youngsters had learned to ring the bells. In the end it was decided that I would have to stop doing this, for fear that I might do something detrimental to my eye. What a shame, I had been stopped yet again from doing something that I really enjoyed taking part in. This seems to be a reoccurring tale throughout my life, whatever I've enjoyed doing; it's immediately taken away from me whether I like it not!

By around 1967 we'd been in the pub for some time, and of course I'd got to know the local people. There was one particular family that we knew very well; they were the Saunders family. These people had owned a little West Highland white terrier bitch, this little dog had managed to get out of the house one day, and a few weeks later they found that she was in pup. Bernie Saunders had been asking in the pub if anybody might be interested in having a puppy, and my parents wanted to know if I'd like one. I of course was so happy at the thought of having my own puppy, and couldn't wait for them to be born. A few days after the event happened, I was asked if I would like to see the puppies. I was going to have the first choice of the litter. We don't know what type of dog the father was, but these pups looked just like Cairn terriers. I know that I choose the smallest out of the litter and eagerly awaited the day when I could go and collect her. At last the day arrived and I brought her home. I called her Brandy. This little dog was to be with me for many years and I really adored her. I'll always remember the first night she spent at home. I'd been to the village shop and had asked if they could give me a large cardboard box that I could put her in as we hadn't got a proper bed. I left her in the sitting room and went off to bed. I'd not been up there very long when she started to howl. She cried all night, and I was so worried by this that I eventually went downstairs to sit with her, but I then began to feel tired so decided to take her up into my bedroom. I would expect that she had missed her mother as it took several nights for her to get used to this. Brandy was such a character and everyone loved her.

One particular thing we noticed after we'd had her for a couple of years was that she was your typical terrier dog. She used to sit by a sheet of corrugated tin each day in the garden under the trees and we wondered what she was up to. I watched her closely, and you would keep seeing her head turn from side to side as if she was listening for something. I thought it was about time I went to investigate and see what she was up to. I walked over to the sheet of metal and lifted it up, only to find this large rat that came rushing out! My little dog made a dive for the rat, but unfortunately this rodent had got hold of her by the nose, she was shrieking in agony and the rat didn't seem to let go. I was so concerned as to what I could do, and tried to pick up a piece of wood in the hope that I might be able to get the rat off her nose. Eventually the rat had released her from its horrendous grip, and before I knew what had happened my little dog had grabbed the rat again, and was shaking the living daylights out of this animal, it just didn't stand a chance; it lay dead on the ground.

Now I'm not keen on rats, but I felt really sorry to think my dog had done this. I suppose it's just something that terriers are known for, but I think it was the first and the last rat she ever killed. I wouldn't have liked her to do this again, as it frightened me so much, not only for the fact that my dog had got hurt, but also to think she had killed another animal.

The Waggon, as it was usually called, had a brilliant darts team and held quite a good position within the leagues that it played. For several years they became one of the best in the area. Darts nights were always busy; some of the wives of the husbands who played darts would come and help Mother prepare sandwiches for the evening. There was such a lovely atmosphere in this little pub, with always something going on. Saturday nights were especially the crowd-puller. We used to have a piano in the pub, and a lady by the extraordinary name of Mrs. Key would come and play. A fixing was made for an organ to be placed just under the piano keyboard and she would play this in conjunction with the piano. People used to come from miles around to hear this and have a sing-song. Those were lovely old days, and everybody so friendly, the pub packed to capacity, plenty of beer flowing and locals, friends and family having a wonderful time.

Our local farmer and landowner used to give me a lift back to Thompson School as her son also went there. I had always got on well with her and her family. Her husband originally came from one of the communist countries and he was great fun to be with. I remember one summer holiday that my friends and I decided to go fishing. There was a great little pit on one of the farmer's pieces of land, all the lads decided to get together one late afternoon to go out for a great afternoon's sport. We sat ourselves down, and had been catching an odd fish or two, when we noticed that landowners were out for a stroll on their property, they made a bee-line for us fishing in their pit. The husband asked me how I was doing and I said quite well, but it was another thing when his wife came up to me. "What do you think you are doing?" she said. I of course replied "Fishing". This wasn't meant to be rude or cheeky in any way, but she just wasn't very happy that we were on her land. I was quite shocked by the way she went on at me and I packed up my gear and I remember running all the way home back to the pub.

I told Mother that we had been caught fishing on the owner's land, and had been severely reprimanded by her for having been there without permission. I said to my mother that I thought that she would be coming down to the pub to tell my parents, and that I was going out to get away from another ear-bashing. True to my word, she turned up at the pub to have a go at Mum and Dad. My parents said that I should stay in, but I wasn't going to have that as I knew that I was going to get wrong all over again when the summer holiday was finished, as I had to be picked up by her again for the school run.

This didn't ever put us off going on her land again. One day all of the lads, including my younger brother Adrian, got together and went walking. We were crossing one of her fields again, and had noticed a load of bullocks grazing on the land. The bullocks saw us on the field, and I expect they thought that we had come to feed them; all of a sudden the herd came running after us. My poor brother was left behind. We had all clambered up into the trees, but Adrian was left on the ground with the bullocks fast approaching. We managed to haul him up the tree. After a while the herd gradually drifted off and we made our escape. This was definitely the last time we trespassed on her land.

I must have been around eight or nine years of age when started to notice people staring at me. This was a bit of a challenge, as they began to look more intently than ever before, it was then I realised that I was quite different from the others. Neither my family nor my friends had ever made an issue of my disfigurement, but now this seemed different. Over time, I found that I was able to judge people's reactions when they first saw me, I knew when someone was finding it difficult to take in the fact that my face was different from the rest.

I have not always been the outward-going person that I am at this present time, and found it very difficult to cope with the looks from people when they first saw me. This was going to be one of the hardest lessons to learn, and in the next two years I was to move from the Primary School up to the Secondary Modern in Watton, which was in the next nearest town to where I lived. This was awful for me at first, but my personality began to shine through and I soon gained lots of friends, in fact it was the start of a long learning process. I would be able to show others that you can turn a negative situation in to a positive one just by being confident in one self.

While we were living at the Waggon, Mum and Dad used to hold a Christmas party for the local children and this was always well attended, they also held bonfire nights too. All of my friends used to get together and collect all the old furniture, wood and anything else that would burn, and build a great bonfire.

Each of the parents would bring their kids with their own fireworks, Dad would buy loads himself too, and we would have a great evening. Hotdogs and burgers, sandwiches and drinks were there for all to enjoy. One particular bonfire night, when everyone had gone home and the fire was almost out, my young brother Adrian decided that he and his mate would set the hollow tree alight which was just down from the bonfire site. I don't think he realised how bad this fire was going to be. The flames were leaping high into the air and the sparks were flying. As far as my poor father was concerned, it was that some sparks from the bonfire that had set this alight. Poor Dad was running backwards and forwards with buckets of water trying to put this burning tree out. I think he must have spent quite a lot of the late evening trying to get this fire under control, but it wasn't until the next day that it was out fully. It was several years later that my brother told him what had actually happened, and I think they both laughed the whole matter off. In fact we still talk about this today, and it still makes us laugh.

LONDON HOSPITALS

By late 1967 my eye problems worsened, and by 1968 I had been referred to Moorfield's Eye Hospital, City Road, in London. I remember the day that I went off to London to Moorfields; my parents took me in the car. It was such a long drive, but we eventually reached our destination. The hospital seemed so strange; it was like going back in time, to around the Victorian days. There were these large rooms, and in these rooms were desk type tables, in fact these reminded me of something straight out of a Dickensian novel, something like "A Christmas Carol" with Ebenezer Scrooge.

We waited until it was my turn to see a consultant. It must have been about one and half hours waiting time and we eventually saw a doctor. The consultant said that they would like to make an appointment for me to come into the hospital for some tests, and so my parents agreed and the specialist said that we would hear in due course. Several weeks went by and a letter duly arrived from the Moorfields. I believe I was to go in the late summer. The days soon came round and it was time for me to go off to the hospital. I would be put under the care of a leading professor at the Moorfields.

During my first few days at Moorfield's I underwent several x-rays, scans and other examinations to find out what may have caused my eye condition. The professor seemed to think that there may also have been an underlying problem because of my height; I had always been quite a short lad for my age. He suggested that I should be transferred to Hammersmith Hospital for tests, to see why I wasn't growing, however I wasn't too keen on going to this place. My father had been staying in London at my aunt's house and was told that he could accompany me to the other hospital; my aunt would be allowed to come along too.

I was taken from Moorfields by hospital transport; it was an old ambulance. I remember that we stopped in one particular area to pick up an old lady. What a fright I had on that day! This old girl got in the ambulance and she was crying; she said that somebody had assaulted her with a knife. I was already scared about having to go to another hospital, let alone being confronted by that old lady saying that she had been attacked. We arrived at Hammersmith. I cried my heart out, as I didn't want to be there. The nurses had put me into a room with all sorts of strange equipment; the room had various bits of machinery. The apparatus that we saw had flashing lights and was also making weird sounds. My aunt insisted that I wasn't staying in that room, and if they didn't move me into a ward she would be taking me home. I was put into a small ward with three other people; this seemed to settle me down a little better than I had been when I first arrived.

Dad stayed around with me most of that afternoon and then a doctor turned up, he said that he wanted to do a test on me. My father said that he would go, but the doctor said that it would only be about 10 minutes. This doctor took me off to another room, and I was absolutely scared out of my wits. I asked him what he was going to do but he really didn't explain at all. I had no idea what was going to happen. He told me that I had to strip off and that I was to lie on the bed with my knees right up to my chin. The next thing was that he had got this two-fingered rubber glove and he was putting Vaseline on it, he then stuck his finger up my bottom! I was absolutely disgusted, what the hell was he up to? It really hurt me. I now of course know that he was doing, it was an investigation to find my prostate gland; this was to check for any abnormalities. The Doctor should have at least explained what this examination was for, especially to a young lad. It had been a very harrowing experience for me. I eventually went back to the ward to see my Dad but I was too embarrassed to say anything about this dreadful nightmare. I can laugh about it now, but at the time this was a terrible ordeal for me.

That evening I cried again. I was so frightened and wanted to be out of that hospital and home with my mother as quickly as possible. The night-time seemed to last forever but, as they daybreak came, the nurses came round and said that I wasn't to have anything to eat at all. I was told that I had to drink as many pints of water as I possibly could. Every time I went to go for a pee this had to be collected, measured and tested. This lasted for several hours. At last this ordeal was over; but what else were they going to throw at me? Evening meal turned up at last but the day had taken its toll on me. I expect it was because I had been drinking water for most of that morning and I had no appetite at all, I just didn't want anything else. I went off to bed early that evening, and I think I must have slept all of that night as I was totally worn out. I had no idea what was planned for the next day.

The breakfast arrived the following morning and I actually managed to eat something. I was starving because I hadn't eaten for a couple of days. Within a couple of hours of having my breakfast the nurse came round to tell me that I was going to have more tests that day. She told me that the doctor would be coming round with some students to discuss my case. I thought this would be OK, but I was in for yet another shock when they all arrived. There must have been two doctors, and three students, two of them being female. They drew the curtains and the consultant asked me to remove my pyjamas, not just the top but the bloody bottom as well! Can you imagine how I felt? A young man just reaching puberty and having to stand stark naked in front of all these people! I was so embarrassed; how could they do this to someone? This was really cruel; I needed my dad so badly but didn't know how to get him. At last I thought this traumatic experience was over, but more tests were to come. That afternoon a Canadian doctor came to see me. He said that they needed to do more investigations. I had to lie in bed while they were taking my blood, injecting something into me. I felt like a pin cushion. I must have had at least about twelve needles into me. By late afternoon it was over and my father arrived. I told him everything about this upsetting experience and said that I wasn't going through any more. He had to get me out of that terrible hospital and as soon as possible. Father immediately phoned my mother; she told him that she would get in touch with my local GP.

Dr Mary Shanks had been my doctor since I was born. Mother told her of what had been going on and asked what they ought to do. Should they let the doctors carry on with these tests or would it be wise to let Dad bring me home? Dr

Mary, as we always called her, said that they should let me make the decision as to what I should do and that I could choose what should happen next. Mum phoned the hospital to tell Father what had been discussed. Within a short while I had packed my belongings and was on my way back. Good riddance to that awful place, never ever again would I go through all that pain and embarrassment? Or at least I thought not. I was taken back to Moorfields but at least my Dad was there with me. Later on, that afternoon, we made our way back home to Norfolk. This had been a really bad trip to hospital, and it took several weeks to settle back to some sort of a normal life again.

Several weeks went by and Hammersmith hospital sent the results of the tests to my doctor. My parents were called in to the surgery and were told that I could have a course of growth hormone injections to try to make me gain some height. Unbeknown to my mum and dad, it was said that those hormones were extracted from the pituitary gland of dead people. In some cases it had been known to cause various issues and side effects, but I wasn't going to be a guinea pig, and decided that I would not have this done. It was only just recently that my mother told me about what they had actually found out from these investigations, and it wasn't what I had been expecting.

Quite a bit of research has been done in recent of years and it has actually shown that it was a bit of a gamble in the use of human hormones. Creutzfeldt-Jakob Disease (C.J.D.) has been mentioned in some cases, even now there is no knowing what terrible things can become of this. I am so glad I didn't go through with these injections, I think that probably it was the fear of the needles that stopped me having it done! Who knows, I might not even have been here writing this story? About a year went by, and at that time I had been experiencing problems with my eye again. Moorfield's hadn't been in touch since my trip to Hammersmith hospital so I went back to my GP to discuss my problems, she organised that I should return to the eye hospital.

On one of my many visits to Moorfield's, I was transferred for more tests to be carried out to find out more about the mass of veins that causes so many problems with my eye, head and mouth; my visit was to be at the National Hospital in Queen's Square, London. When I arrived I was taken into the X-ray department by one of the nurses. She asked if I had been told what was going to happen? I said that there had been mention of a small injection. The nurse soon told me of the procedure, and said that quite an extensive examination would take place, it was to be an angiogram. This didn't mean anything to me until I was actually laid on a table with three or four people in attendance.

The doctor then explained what was going to happen. I was to have an incision made in my right arm with a scalpel. This was to be done with no anaesthetic whatsoever. I couldn't believe what he was telling me. He then said that they would insert a catheter tube through my artery and into my heart. I felt like getting up and running away from there. The doctor started this procedure. The pain of the scalpel cutting into my arm was horrifying; I could see the blood dripping off my arm and onto the floor from this incision. I was crying in pain, and asked if I could have anaesthetic, they said no. They then started passing this tube up through the blood vessel in my arm. I started to cry and again I asked whether I could have anaesthetic, and yet again they said no. The only way I can explain the dreadful pain that I was going through is to say that it felt as if hot poker was being pushed up into my arm, it was excruciating. In all of this time the nurses were holding me down on the table and there was no escape from this torture. As I lay there, I watched the tube on the X-ray screen. They used this screen to guide this tube through the artery and up into my heart.

At last it was in position. They then explained to me that the catheter was being connected to a pump, this would deliver a fluorescein dye to the heart and then of course my heart in turn would pump the dye around the body and to the head, so that a picture could be taken to see where all the irregular veins were in and around my eye. At last, the angiogram was over, the tube had to come back out. I went through all the pain again as this was removed. I have never experienced anything as agonizing as this before in my life. I have had all sorts done to me throughout the years and have taken it all with a pinch of salt, but this was horrendous. A few weeks later after having had the angiogram done, I saw my surgeon. I asked him what he had found out from this test. He told me that he hadn't come to any conclusions after having this done, I did really feel angered by this, all of that pain, and for absolutely nothing! I was taken back to Moorfields where, later that afternoon, I was discharged from hospital.

I will however always be indebted to my surgeons John Wright and Geoffrey Rose, John has been retired for several years now. He saw the need for me to have some kind of corrective surgery and carried out all of these operations in those early years. Way back in 1994 I was admitted to Moorfields to have yet another operation; I went down to the theatre as normal, full of the joys of spring in the hope that this would help me with my ongoing condition. I thought it would be great to tidy up some of these veins again on my eyelids. Later that afternoon I woke up in the ward to find myself on a plasma drip. Within about an hour or so of waking up in the ward my surgeon came to see me. "David" he said, "you had us worried down there". I asked, ' What did he mean? " He said that I had had a severe hemorrhage. "We had a bit of a job stopping the bleeding". I must admit I did feel rough.

When talking to this medical man I remarked about this operation, mentioning about the hemorrhage. He turned to me and said that it was nothing unusual for me, as it usually happened in my case. I can quite honestly tell you, it does worry me a bit more that it used to, as I just seemed to sail through all of this when I was a younger man and in my prime. In all the years that I have been attending the hospital, it's been an endless stream of operations, to tell you the truth I think I've lost count now regarding the number of times that I've had procedures done. I do feel really grateful though as they have tried to help as much as they could especially with such the rare condition that I have, I don't know what I would have done without them, even with all the pain that's been associated with this.

AND SO TO TOWN

My schooling years ended and my parents decided that it would be a good idea for them to move into a large town and to a bigger pub, we were going to King's Lynn. I wasn't sure that I wanted to go, but this wasn't up to me. My parents took over another tenancy, this was a much larger public house; it was called "The Princess Royal" and was situated in Blackfriars Street. We had moved from the quietness of a lovely little village of a few hundred people, to the bustling town of King's Lynn where several thousand inhabitants live. Please believe me, this was a reality shock; that comfortable little world that I had lived in for such a long time had come to an end so suddenly. Here I was, a village lad, going to what seemed to be like a big city. I didn't know whether I was going to cope with it all. This move was to be something totally different from the small family pub that we had lived in, and somewhere that I began to encounter the nastier side of life.

Adrian, my brother, was to attend St. James's School; he was seven years younger than I. It was decided that I would have to collect Adrian from school each day as Mum and Dad would be running their business. I knew in my own mind that there was going to be some problems regarding this, as I'd already experienced the intense staring that had taken place since moving to King's Lynn.

Each afternoon I would get worked up inside, about having to go to the school. I knew that some of the children would come out of the playground taunting me, they would be calling me names. There were also other people would stare at me, it was as if I were something out of a the ordinary, it was truly an awful time. I had never known people to be like this before, this totally blew any confidence that I had, and I found it extremely difficult at times. I found it near impossible to look at people straight in their eyes for fear of their reaction to my looks. In fact I would walk around with my hand over my face or even wear a pair of dark glasses to cover my disfigurement. I only wanted to be treated normally like any other person, but this was a very difficult thing for some people to do, they just wouldn't accept me and my looks.

When we first moved to King's Lynn, I wasn't allowed to work as my doctors had said that I might do something detrimental to my condition. I was put onto a disablement benefit, and was given a booklet to collect money at the post office every week; this lasted for about 18 months. One day I decided that enough was enough, and I wasn't going to have this any longer, all I wanted to do was to get a job and to be independent. I went to the Benefits Office and handed my booklet in. When I got home and told my parents of my decision, my father hit the roof. What the hell had I done? I was now without any money and didn't even have a job. Of course I knew that my parents were the kind of people who cared very much about me anyway, whatever the circumstances; they weren't about to throw me out in the street. I went to the Employment Agency as it was called then. I was introduced to the Disablement Officer and told him of my condition and what I had done regarding my benefits. He said not to worry, as he was almost certain that he would find me employment. Within a few days I'd had a phone call from him saying that I could have an interview for a position at food refrigeration processing factory. I went to the interview and was accepted for the position as a Quality Control Inspector; the manager was very keen for me to get started, but said there was a probability of me having to do shift work. I wasn't too keen on the idea, but decided that I would give it a try. Unfortunately I only lasted there for a few weeks; I found the shifts to be a bit hard on my medical condition as it was affecting my eye too badly.

I happened to have a friend who was an under-manager for a food retail supermarket and asked him if there were any jobs going. Luckily enough they were taking people on and I left my left my job at the refrigeration company on the Friday and started in the shop on the Monday. This position was to put me back in the spotlight of people once again. Obviously working in this environment I would have to meet and talk to people, and I found this to be very challenging. I started on the shop floor, I then learned how to run the wines and spirits department, I did a spell in the greengrocery department and was eventually trained to work in the provisions department.

Gradually over time I again met new friends and learned that it was quite easy just to be myself and the rest would happen for me. I have always been quite lucky in the fact that people who I got to know liked me and have been blessed with an enormous amount of true friendship that most people would envy. This friendship has been one of the most important things in my life and which I value most.

Although having all of these friends, I was still a very lonely young man. I wanted the companionship of a girlfriend, but no girl would accept me with the disfigurement that I had. There was one particular girl I really fancied; she worked in one of the supermarkets down the road from where we lived. She used to come in the pub most weekdays in her dinner break but just I didn't have the nerve to ask her out. A friend and I happened to go out for a drink one evening and would you believe it, that particular girl that I fancied was there in the pub. I told my mate of how I'd felt about her, and during the course of the evening this so called friend asked her out himself. What a rotten mate he was! How could someone who I thought was a real friend do this to me? I was just a fool, I should have kept my mouth shut! A few days later she finished with him, this cheered me up, but I still hated him for doing this to me. Several weeks later I plucked up courage to ask her out, but she flatly refused me; I could see and even feel her repulsion to my looks. This really made me feel so bad, and had a terrible effect on me for several years to come; I wouldn't even try to ask any girl out any more for fear of getting the same reaction. I always remember my dad trying to make me feel better about myself, and he would come out with this old saying, "A faint heart never won a fair maiden". This still didn't help me and I struggled for years to gain the nerve to ask someone ever again.

Working in a supermarket had several advantages though; there were several other girls there of the same age as myself, and I began to form friendships with them, but this was purely on a 'good friend' basis. I think this was quite helpful to me as this built up my broken confidence. My work in the shop was great and I enjoyed my position within the provisions department. There were three floors to the building that we worked in. The ground floor was the main food shopping area of the business, while on the second floor they sold clothes, white goods and home furnishings etc. The provisions preparation room was situated on the very top floor. Each of the provisions staff had to take a turn in doing one late night per week, mine being on Thursdays. Every night, before finishing off work we would have to take all of the sliced cooked meat from the counter to the top floor to be put in the chilled fridges. On one particular Thursday evening, I had loaded up a trolley with all of these foods ready to be sent up on the dumb waiter (a small lift). This small trolley would just fit inside the lift. John, was our provisions manager he had already pressed the button for this lift to come down, and I stood waiting beside him to put the trolley inside.

What a shock I had in store! The lift arrived, I opened the door and instead of me putting the trolley into the lift, I was pushed in, the door was shut and the next thing I knew was that I heading upward two floors in complete darkness. The lift came to a sudden halt so I began to kick the door, I'd hoped that I was at least at the very top level of the building. The door opened, and there stood the butchery manager and he gave me a right rollicking. I said that it wasn't my fault but I wouldn't own up to who the person was who had put me in there. It seems very funny now, but it was a very dangerous thing to have done. Just a few months ago I was talking with a friend whom I had worked with at the store, we had been chatting about old times and about the lift fiasco. I was quite shaken to find out that few weeks later, after I had finished working there, the lift had plummeted from the top floor down to the bottom! That's frightening!

During my time of working for this supermarket, I was sent away to Cambridge on a training course, this was to learn the skills of bacon preparation. I hated every minute of this. I had never been away on courses, doing anything like this before, and at the end of the four days' intensive training we were to take an exam. I think everyone apart from me got marks in the top 80's and 90's. I was quite embarrassed as think I only scored about 77 percent. I was quite worried by this. My course tutor spoke to me afterwards and said that it wasn't a big deal because he had had others before me who hadn't even scored that, it still worried me though. I got back into the routine again, and from that time on I think I progressed quite well until, one day I made a bit of a slip-up. When you're boning out meat and bacon you are really supposed to wear a hard protective plastic apron; this particular day I wasn't. I was boning out a side of bacon and had removed all of the relevant bones ready to split down into joints for stringing up and also for slicing. As I was pulling the large 14-inch steak knife towards myself; the knife slipped and went straight into my leg, I immediately realised that I'd stabbed myself. I casually walked into the butchery department which was next door, as I knew that the manager knew about first aid. In a rather half-hearted voice he said, "What have you done now?" I said I had stabbed my leg. "Drop your trousers," he said. I was quite a shy sort of bloke and said I wasn't too bothered, "Stop being silly! was his answer", I need to know what you've done." I let him look, and he bandaged my leg as it had been bleeding quite badly. He then took me off to the casualty department of the hospital, where I was examined and asked lots of questions as to how this had happened. Luckily, I had missed a main artery and the cut wasn't as bad as first feared. I was tidied up, given a couple of injections and told to watch what I was doing in the future. In the years that I had done bacon preparation I had cut myself several times, especially on my hands, but that was all part of the job really.

While living at The Princess Royal, we seemed to attract quite a few of the younger drinkers. When I say younger drinkers I don't mean under-age; these young people were around the 18 to 25 year age groups. They were so respectful to my parents, and we never had any trouble from them. My parents treated them as if they were their own, and I am sure this is the reason why they were so respectful back. George was one of these youngsters, he was my real mate; we used to go everywhere together. One night George said to me that we were going to take a ride out to Fair Green, near Middleton. He said that his girlfriend was learning to drive, so we would go as far as The Gate public house, she could then take over in having a drive of his Morris 1000 car.

I can't remember his girlfriends name but she bought along a mate too so there were four of us in the motor. We got as far as the junction, off of the main road from Lynn to Swaffham, he pulled over, and then his girlfriend got in the driving seat. George obviously sat beside her. I sat behind his girlfriend and the other girl was sitting beside me. His girlfriend started to drive away, and as you can probably guess; she stalled the car. I don't think she'd driven that much beforehand although after a while she eventually gained some confidence. George gave her more encouragement by saying that she was doing fine. We were going along rather nicely now, but both George and I knew that a sharp right-hand bend was coming up. George asked her if she was using the footbrake to compensate for the sharp bend, "Of course I am she replied," but in actual fact she had put her foot on the accelerator. We hit the corner doing about forty miles an hour. We went straight through the hedge and into the dyke behind! It was as if everything was happening in slow motion. George had loads of paperwork on his back window, and this was thrown all over the place through the car. The fastening that holds the driving seat to the floor had broken, and as we came to an abrupt halt the seat went forward riding up the front of my legs. I was bleeding and it really hurt badly. George shouted to everyone to ask if we were OK, everyone seemed fine apart from me and my legs. Luckily the car had wedged into a hawthorn bush as it went down the bank, luckily this had stopped us going further down into the water in the dyke. We all managed to get out of the car, but somebody who had been driving behind us saw what had happened. He had stopped to see if anybody had been injured, and if there was anything he could do, but I didn't say a word about being hurt.

I was beginning to get concerned because my parents were always worrying over me, I wasn't going to get back home in time before the pub shut, and alarm bells would be ringing in their minds over me. I asked George if it was alright for me to try and get back home. Fortunately the man in the car that had stopped behind us said that he was going back into King's Lynn and that I could have a lift. George agreed that I couldn't do anything to help in getting the motor out of the dyke but he was also worried that he'd be in trouble if my parents found out what had happened. Before I left, we all agreed not to mention a thing to anyone about our eventful evening, of what had happened to us on that night.

We eventually arrived in King's Lynn; the man who had given me a lift dropped me off just outside the pub. I was limping and my legs were still bleeding slightly. It was half past eleven and the door was bolted when I knocked on the door. I thought I had better try to hide the limp that I had acquired, and to make sure that no-one could see any blood on my trousers. Mother opened up the door and mentioned to me that I had been a bit late in getting home, however I could see that there were still people left in the pub, this gave me a good excuse to get out of the way and up to the bathroom where I attended to my wounds. Fortunately there were only deep grazes to my legs, so it was just superficial, but they still didn't half hurt! My trousers were bloodied, but I soaked them in the sink and thought of an idea to say that I had got muck over them or something. I never ever mentioned this to my parents what happened to me that evening. I know if I had said anything about it I would never have been able to go out any more with George. He came in the pub a few days later, and told me all about how he got his car home and how he would have to spend quite a bit of money to get it back on the road again. We sat and had a good talk about how lucky we were, but we also both had a good laugh in the end about the Flying Moggy 1000.

A few years went by and George asked me if I would be his best man at his wedding. This was a really lovely gesture from George and of course I agreed. Several weeks passed and the stag-night arrived so we all went out for a drink. His evening was brilliant; we were all legless as we say here in Norfolk, poor George was absolutely sloshed. At the end of the night I said to George, "Will you be alright about getting home". He said he was walking and he'd be fine. I watched as he went on his way. His feet were all over the place but he'd insisted that he would be OK. I met George the next morning, the day of his wedding. He said that he had been sick in the road on the way home. I said, "Never mind George, at least you're here". I said that I hadn't been too good either, but he said, "It's ok for you!" I asked him what he meant but I hadn't realised he had lost his four front false teeth while being ill on the way home. When the wedding photos had been processed a few weeks later we were all rolling about with laughter, poor George had such a brilliant smile, minus his four front false teeth of course.

George was one of the many colourful young people who came into our pub along with many others over the years. He especially, had been a wonderful friend to me. In fact, all of the young people who used the pub became some of the best friends that I'd ever made. We all hung out together, whenever there was a good band on at the Corn Exchange we would all be there. In the early 70's all the big bands used to come to King's Lynn and we made sure we saw them

By the summer of 1976 my parents had left the pub trade to retire due to my Dad's ill health .

ON THE MOVE AGAIN

We moved to a little town house in the centre of King's Lynn but it seemed so strange to be out of the pub life after all those years. The house was in a terraced row; it was just like living in "Coronation Street". This was a rented property, and my parents had spent lots of money in doing the inside of the house up, there hadn't been anybody living in it for quite some time. New gas fires were installed, the house was redecorated and new carpets were fitted throughout. We lived there for about eighteen months but Mum and Dad couldn't stick the quietness any longer. My parents felt absolutely lost, the feeling of being away from the pub life was awful, they had enjoyed being in the company of people so much. It was then that they decided to take over yet another public house, this was The Black Horse. This time it would mean being back out in the country again, they would move to a large village called Clenchwarton. Mum and Dad asked me if I would like to work for them. I agreed to this and so a new era in my life began.

Every day, two or three girls who lived in the village came into the pub for their dinner breaks; they were workers from one of the local shops. They were really smashing girls and treated with the most wonderful respect. I felt so at ease with them as they accepted me for who I was and not what I looked like. I think it was because of them that I gradually learned to build up such an amazing self-belief with the opposite sex again; it was the first time that I had been treated like this and gave me such a fantastic feeling of confidence. Those girls, along with loads of other people that

I met while we lived in Clenchwarton still remain friends to this very day. It's now thirty two years or so on and I see them from time to time at parties that we get invited to. I value all these people so much for the friendships which were formed, especially for what they did for me all those years ago.

The village of Clenchwarton was quite a hive of activity. There was always something going on in this community, including fancy dress nights in the local village hall, village dances, fetes and several fundraising events. I had some great times in this brilliant village and the parties I used to go to were something else. I can remember being invited to Rod's house; Rod was having a bottle party so I went. I must have got there about nine o'clock that evening, I'd already been on the beer in the pub before we went. I vaguely remember going with Keith; we were both well on the way for being half drunk before we got to the party, but Rod welcomed us in with open arms. He was a great chap and he loved his beer too. Boy did we have a excellent night, the drinks just kept flowing. The drink was beginning to get the better of me as I was feeling a bit worse for the wear. I would think it was around one o'clock in the morning and said my farewells to everyone. However I managed to stagger home, I'll never know how I got there, but I did. Unfortunately, Mum and Dad had locked up, they must have gone off to bed. I tried banging on the door to get in as I hadn't got a key. Nobody heard me; I tried again but to no avail. What was I going to do now? A great idea came into my head; we had an old shed outside that our German Shepherd dog used to be in during the day time, this was enclosed by a chain-linked run. I got inside the shed with intentions of kipping down for the night as it was lined out with straw. I must have laid there for about a quarter of an hour and found that I was getting cold. I went back to the front of the house and banged on the door again, but nobody came.

The thought of being locked out, being cold and having to sleep in the dog shed all night must have sobered me up, then I had a brainwave. I went back to Rod's house and the party was still in full swing. I couldn't face another drink, but asked Rod if I could use his telephone to ring mum and dad to let them know I was on the way home. I rang, and I can assure you the reception from them was like the weather outside, it was very frosty. I got the third degree when I got back! That put me off drink and parties for quite a while, until the next time so to speak.

I worked for Mum and Dad for about a couple of years at the Black Horse, and then decided that I needed my independence yet again. I asked one of the customers who used to come and drink in the pub if he might know of any jobs coming up in the factory where he worked. Don was the works manager at a pen factory, and he told me that he would be taking on people in a few weeks and he would let me know nearer the time. A couple of months went by and I was asked to attend an interview with him, this went quite well, and he decided to give me a month's trial. The month soon flew by, and they seemed happy with my work, and so I was taken on by the company. There were several sections within this factory and I started in the colours department. This mainly entailed making solid and water-based paint for schools. I moved around within this section doing various duties. Obviously I was still living at home with my parents in the pub so I still enjoyed my social life. There was only one problem of living in a place of this nature, the temptation to drink was quite overpowering, especially being with my mates, I couldn't be off having a few beers.

On one particular day I went to work, I had been on the beer the previous evening and I really shouldn't have been driving the next day, as I felt quite under the weather. Andrew, my boss, asked me to fill about a hundred pots of finger paint. These were containers that were about the size of half a jam jar. The finger paint had already been made, and stored in large containers, something of the size of an oil drum. It was a bit of an old fashioned way of doing things, but these small pots were filled manually. You would use a large ladle, and when you got to the very base of the drum you would have to reach further into the very bottom to get the remaining paint out. How I never fell into the drum that day I will never know! I was already standing on something to give me a bit of height and I just felt I was going in. Can you imagine me with my head down in the bottom of this barrel with my legs sticking out. Luckily I managed to get myself standing upright again and no worse for wear.

About two years went by and I applied for another job within the factory; this particular job was in a department where all the pen barrels were printed and assembled. A new machine had been imported from Italy, and I was to be the operator to learn how to work it. This was a bad move on my part, and I was to find out how hard this new job was about to be. The new machine arrived; it was enormous and was initially made for printing cola cans. The people who worked in the machinery department had to mill the spindles on this piece of equipment down to a pen-barrel size. This really didn't work quite properly, and I had terrible trouble in keeping this device working all the hours to produce the amount of printed barrels that were needed. These would then be taken onto the production line for assembly to make the pens. In the end I had to give this job up because of stress that took a terrible toll on my health. Fortunately for me, another job came up within the factory, which I then applied for. I did indeed get this position. This was a totally stress-free job, and from then on I thoroughly enjoyed being at this factory.

Meeting Joanne

It was the week leading up to the Bank Holiday of August 1983 that I had been invited to a friend's barbeque birthday party. Mandy, one of my dear friends, who I'd known for several years thought it would be a good idea to get me out from my usual routine.. It was nothing unusual for me to sit in the pub with my mates drinking away the hours and perhaps even feeling sorry for myself, so she asked me to her party. That night, when she'd asked me to go, I thought it would be great idea and was getting quite excited about the prospect of having an evening out for a change.

As the week had progressed, my little dog was taken very ill, so I decided that I wasn't going to attend the party. Brandy had reached the great old age of nineteen. We had taken her to the vet's as she had been so poorly, it just so happened to be on this particular party weekend. The vet had told us that she'd probably had a stroke, he'd given her some injections along with some other medication, he explained that it would be touch and go as to whether she would survive. In my mind, there was no way that I'd be going out partying, especially when my poor little dog was so ill, I was going to stay with her whatever the circumstances. Peter, a friend of mine, had turned up at the pub to pick me up to take me to the party. My mother was behind the bar serving. Peter had asked her if I were ready and she had tried to explain the situation? Mother tried to call me, but our living quarters were above the pub. It was quite hard to hear anyone in the downstairs bars, especially if the television was turned on upstairs, so I hadn't answered. The next thing I knew was that Mum came up the stairs to see where I was, she mentioned that Peter was here to take me to the party. I told her that I wouldn't go as I was staying with my dog but I went down to the bar to have a word with him. Peter wasn't having any of this as he had other ideas, he said that I had no choice in the matter and that I was going whether I liked it or not. So reluctantly I got myself dressed up, and off we went in the car. It's strange how things happen you know? It was on that particular evening that I meet my future wife.

We got to the party and sat with our friends. As usual, some of them had girlfriends. I felt absolutely lost and into the bargain I'd been thinking about my little dog. My friend Mandy, came up to me and said that she wanted me to meet someone. Mandy introduced me to Joanne; I sat with her for some time talking;. I found out during our conversation that Joanne had been born profoundly deaf so she too also knew what it was like to be lonely. We sat talking most of the evening and seemed to hit it off quite well. I left the party later that evening, but hadn't even tried to arrange to meet Joanne again for fear that I would be turned down. I felt terrible that I had not asked Joanne for any contact information; I was beginning to think we could have perhaps made a date to see each other again. A few days later I plucked up some courage and called round to see Mandy to enquire if she'd ask Joanne if she might like to go out for a drink or something. To my astonishment, Mandy had made an arrangement for Joanne to meet me. Joanne had never actually been out with anybody before and I was someone who had tried to date other girls unsuccessfully. All of the other girls in the past that I'd asked to date, were looking for somebody who was "normal", as the saying goes. This had all been so very hard for me in the past, and of course I felt so wary, I dearly needed companionship, I needed someone who would love me for what I was and not what I looked like, I felt that Joanne was that person. She took me for the person I was inside and did not judge me one bit by my looks. She was and still is one of the greatest people that I have ever met in my life and I love her very deeply.

Unfortunately, on the weekend that I met Joanne my little dog died. I feel that this meeting with Joanne was meant to be, and this was something that was inevitably going to happen. Within the next few days I met Joanne again and we went off to the cinema. That was a night to remember! The film showing that evening was E.T. but unfortunately we had arrived a bit late. In the opening sequence of this film it's set in pitch darkness. The usher in the cinema was trying to show us where some seats were with her torch. As you can imagine, everyone has to stand up especially when the spare seats are further down the line. I went first and thought I'd found an empty seat, but to my horror I sat on a blokes lap, he wasn't too amused I'll tell you. How embarrassing this was for me, and I had only known Joanne for this short while too, I felt such an idiot. Whatever did she think of me, making a fool out of myself like that. I can assure you, I didn't live that one down for quite some time.

However, Joanne and I just got on so well and over the following weeks we started to go out with each other. Joanne then invited me home to meet her family. This of course really worried me, as I wondered what sort of reaction I was going to get. I went over for a Sunday lunch and my nerves were terrible. David and Jean, Joanne's parents were so good with me and accepted me straight away, it was such a wonderful feeling to be accepted as quickly as this. I'm sure think that they probably realised how Joanne had been so lonely; it was good that she had met somebody who also knew what it was like to be in the same position.

Going out with Joanne didn't seem real at first, and I never thought it would ever happen to me, but our love for each other grew day by day. We were going with each other for about three years and then decided that it was time to get married. Our family and friends were overjoyed and all I wanted to do was to tell the world about it. This was the most exciting thing that had ever happened in my life. Of course I told everyone of the forthcoming event. One day, as I was clocking off work, I approached one of the ladies whom I used to pass as I was leaving. I told her of my forthcoming marriage to Joanne. This lady turned to me and said, "I didn't think anybody would want to marry someone with a face looking like that." I was totally gob-smacked at how cruel this person had been to me. I couldn't believe the words that came out of her mouth. I didn't say anything to her about my feelings, but this was just sheer ignorance on her part. I think that if I'd reacted in a negative way to this and perhaps have said something, I would only have been a lowering myself to her level. What she had said to me wasn't exactly the sort of thing you would declare to anyone, disfigured or not, as it was such an awful remark. I feel almost certain that had I not been strong enough, it could have been quite devastating for me. Anyway, I brushed this aside, and decided that it wasn't worth worrying about.

Joanne and I were married on 25th July 1987 at Heacham Church in the village where she lived, the congregation was near to overflowing. This was like one of those stories you read of as a child, a fairy story coming true. We had our reception in the village Public Hall and I think there must have been around three hundred guests. Our honeymoon was spent in Tenerife. Our marriage has brought so much joy to our family and friends and as I write it's now in its twenty-ninth year.

After being married for around three years we thought that it was time to think about having a family. I was so concerned regarding the problem that I had been born with would perhaps be passed on to any children that we might have. I made an appointment to see my surgeon in London to ask his opinion on the matter. We had a private meeting with my then surgeon, Mr John Wright. We were so pleased to find out that it would be a chance in a million for something like this to happen again. On April 10th 1991 at the Queen Elizabeth Hospital in King's Lynn our daughter Lindsay was born. Lindsay is blond-haired and blue-eyed and is now 25 years old. She has grown up to be the kind-hearted caring young lady that everyone would wish for and we totally adore her. She is our pride and joy and has completed our family, a family that I never thought would happen.

In the writing of this chapter I feel that I needed to add an additional note as it's rather poignant to me. In my long journey in trying to find somebody special in my life, I just wanted to say I sincerely thought that this would never come to pass for me. What would happen if I couldn't find someone to love me, how would my life pan out? If only it was true that you could have three wishes in your life, what would happen if those wishes would definitely come true. I expect you've heard of this old story before, and that it's just a load of old hogwash. Well I'm going to tell you something, I was so desperate to find love and I did actually make those three wishes, I had even said them out aloud because I had totally given up of all hope of having a normal life. The three wishes that I speak of are here in writing for all to see.

I wanted to meet a girl who would love me.

I wanted to marry that girl.

I wanted to have a family.

These wishes came true for me, I have always believed that if there's something in life that you want really, really badly and that it hurts you deep down inside you'll get it! I proved that this can happen as it did for me!

POSITIVE THINKING

Today you will find me a very positive person, whereas in the early years it was very hard for me to come to terms that I had this disfigurement. When I walk down a street anywhere these days, the feeling I have is that I am no different from anybody else. People may stare, but it's something that will never go away, so why bother about it? I expect you've heard of the old saying "Like water off of a duck's back", this is how I feel about it myself now. To anybody with a disfigurement who may be reading this today, please believe me when I say that it is of no importance what you look like, it's the person that you are inside. You are no different from the rest, in fact I've often said to myself that I am unique. Just be yourself and you'll find people will see beyond the disfigurement. In my own mind, I would rather that somebody asks me what's happened to your face, it's far better than them saying something negative, something that would have an impact on your life. I have always been willing to explain to a person who wants to know more about my condition. I feel very deeply in my mind that this not only helps me to gain some self-confidence, but it also helps those people who find it difficult to overcome their fear of meeting somebody with a facial disfigurement. Throughout my lifetime I have tried to show people that disfigurement doesn't have to be a thing to be troubled by. Obviously there will always be a few people who cannot cope with this, but that's their problem and not mine. Unfortunately there are still some people who can be really rude, and won't even speak when they are spoken to because they fear something about that person. Other people enquire as to what has happened to my face, but there are those who will make insensitive remarks like, "What does the other bloke look like"! They say some really awful things, but over the years I have become very toughened to these words.

If there's one piece of advice that I could give to someone, it would be this. Please just think about what you're going to say to that person, don't say nasty things, because it can change that person's life in just a few seconds. A few wrong words can have a devastating effect on any one individual for the rest of their lives. I have gone through my life with the intention of trying to make at least one person happy, at least once a day. If you can just do this one thing, you will see your life change in some really remarkable ways. My life has been a roller coaster of a ride, but please believe me, there's been some ups and there's been some downs, but the ups score totally high above all else.

I currently work in a Care Home for old age pensioners and I just totally adore being with these dear people. Some of these individuals have dementia and also Alzheimer's disease but it gives me the greatest pleasure to keep them happy. In the time I've been there that none of these people have ever questioned me about my looks, they take me as I am. My job is so rewarding, I'm what is known as an Activities Co-ordinator, but I believe my main job is that of befriending. All of these very dear people love to have the company of someone who has the time to talk and involve them in things.

In the summing up of this chapter I must just tell you that I have lead a rich and fulfilled life. Gladly the bad days are hard to remember now but it was a very hard journey in the beginning. I now look forward to every day of my life as it's a very happy one. I will always endeavour to be the outward-going person that I am today. If you see me in the street, please come up and introduce yourself, be kind and don't make negative remarks and you'll find that I'll respond to you with the same dignity that you give me.

CHARITY WORK

Over several years I've tried to give some of my spare time to the charity "Changing Faces". Changing Faces is an organisation that I became involved with way back in January 1999 having met a young Chinese man by the name of Simon Tan. I had met with Simon at Moorfields Eye Hospital when my then surgeon had written to me asking if I would meet one of his patients, a young Asian man. Mr Wright had asked if I would be prepared to have a chat with this young chap at the clinic, Simon was interested meeting with someone with a similar condition to that of his own. If I was prepared to do this, the meeting would take place on my annual check-up at the hospital, I said that I would be more than pleased to see him. This meeting was way back in 1995 and we still remain friends and keep in contact after all these years from that of our very first meeting.

A few months after our meeting, Simon mentioned to me something about the charity, Changing Faces. Changing Faces is an organisation that was started way back in 1992 by a man by the name of James Partridge. James saw the need for helping people who suffer with disfigurements of some kind or other, be it on their body, face or hands. James is a wonderful chap, who had the foresight to set up this fantastic charity. This organisation has helped thousands of people including adults, children, young people and their families, to come to terms with these issues, and is willing to talk to anyone who is having problems in learning to cope with disfigurement.

The charity is led by a fantastic team of people who can provide help for individuals, adults, children and families with information or counselling, they can even offer schools advice and training. It's a brilliant organisation that I've been so proud to be part of and I will endeavour to support them in whatever way I possibly can. I have tried to be of assistance and hopefully bringing disfigurement and its issues to the public spotlight. About a thirteen years ago I was asked by the charity if I would be prepared to go on a photo shoot for an advertising campaign that was being organised, this was being arranged by an advertising agency called WCRS in London. WCRS is responsible for some of the well-known advertisements that we regularly see on the television. I agreed to take part, I went to London on Wednesday 18th September 2002 and spent the best part of the day being photographed by a young professional photographer by the name of Andy Flack. Over the next few days three other people were also photographed for this campaign, their names being Michelle Godfrey, Susan Duncan and Mark Crank. Several weeks later we were informed that the campaign was ready for the set go.

My wife and I were then invited by The Duke Of Westminster, James Partridge and the trustees of the charity to a pre-poster launch in Grosvenor Street, London W1 on the evening of Tuesday 12th November 2002. There were a few television personalities including Moira Stewart, former Northern Ireland Secretary Lord King and several advertising and business people from the city on that evening. After speeches by The Duke of Westminster and James Partridge, several of these people came up to me to ask how I had become involved in this campaign, and I was even approached by the actor William Simons (Heartbeat), who is a patron of the charity, he was very interested by the work I had done. This had been a wonderful evening for both Joanne and me and I feel really honoured to have been able to take part in this campaign.

On Monday 16th December James Partridge, who is the Executive Director of Changing Faces, launched the poster campaign in London. These posters were displayed in several prominent places, such as Oxford Street, Knightsbridge, Shaftsbury Avenue, Charring Cross, Buckingham Palace Road and a few other places until Sunday 29th December 2002. James Partridge was interviewed on BBC Breakfast TV and also on the afternoon programme Open House with Gloria Hunniford, regarding the posters and the imminent advertising campaign.

In January 2003 there was media coverage (newspapers and magazines) regarding this campaign, and so the four people involved in it were recognised throughout the country. Following these events there have been several other media projects in which I have been involved. A very nice chap by the name of Mike Liggins interviewed Joanne and me for a local television programme called BBC Look East. This was shown in June 2003. In August of the same year I had a telephone call from the charity to ask me if I might be interested in taking part in a television programme for BBC1, called The Lifeline Appeal. If I was happy to take part, I was to let Changing Faces know as soon as possible. I was ready and willing to do anything like this, and so within a few hours I phoned them to say how keen I would be to take part. They told me that they would get in touch with the producer of the programme, and that she would then get back to me. Two or three days went by and I was contacted by e-mail to arrange a visit from Amanda, the producer. She would come and visit me in my home in Heacham. A date was fixed and she would come and see me on Sunday 21st September. The days couldn't go quick enough, I was so excited at the thought of being on national television.

The Sunday soon came round and Amanda turned up and also with her husband, who happened to be the sound recordist for the programme. Amanda said that we should just talk about my life and what had happened to me over the years. She wanted to get an insight into my life and how I had led it. By the end of our meeting she seemed to be quite interested by my story, but said that I shouldn't build up my hopes as she had other people to see also. I just hoped that they would decide to use me. Amanda told me that she would be getting back in touch within the next couple of weeks or so to let me know if she could use me or not. The days just seemed to drag by and I wasn't sure if she would use me or not? On Monday 13th October I received a call to say that I would be taking part in her film. I was so excited by this and couldn't believe that I would be in a major advertising programme on BBC television. Arrangements were made for someone to meet me at King's Cross Station on Friday 21st November.

I was met me at the station; by the coordinator for documentaries for the BBC and she took me off to a café where we were to meet the film crew. The team turned up and off we went to Euston Road to find one of advertising boards with my poster on it. The crew set up the cameras and were ready to film. I had to walk up and down the road by this large picture of myself while they filmed. It was quite strange to see the reactions of the public to this. The filming must have taken about an hour I think, and I was then told that we would go off for lunch. They took me to a little pub where I was treated to a meal and drinks. They looked after me well, I felt like a film star, and it was really great to be pampered like this. After our meal we would be going to the Changing Faces office that was just round the corner from the pub, and I would then have to talk on film about myself.

      The Changing Faces office at Junction Mews was a small place, and it must have caused quite a bit of a disruption for the people who worked there, with all the camera equipment and lights. I sat waiting in the reception area for my turn to take part. I knew I was to meet the actor Nick Berry, and he was going to present the introduction to the programme. The door opened and he walked in. It was fantastic to meet this man; he was a really great chap and sat talking with me for quite a while until the film crew had set up everything to start filming. They called Nick and he said, 'Come on up and watch while I do my bit.' This only took a short while as Nick had rehearsed his lines. You could tell that he was a professional actor; it was good to see how these people work. It was now my turn to take part in the documentary. Amanda asked me questions relating to my life and how people reacted to me when they saw me. She also asked several other questions concerning how I was affected by the way people treated me. This was all recorded and took around an hour; my part in the film had been done. This would be taken back to be edited and made up for the programme, which would be shown in February of 2004. Nick wished me luck and left the office, and a taxi had been arranged to take me back to King's Cross Station. I said my goodbyes to all the staff at the charity office and got back to King's Cross and also back to some sort of reality again. My day with the film crew was one that I will remember for many years to come, and it was fantastic to meet a real-life actor. On February 8th 2004 the programme was shown on BBC1 to 3.4 million viewers. Another 2.6 million people saw the programme again the following day on BBC2. I am very proud to have been part of this programme, and feel very honoured to have been chosen.

During my time of being involved with Changing Faces I was recorded for the radio on the late John Peel's Radio 4 programme 'Home Truths' talking about disfigurement. I did write a very small article for one of the charity's booklets and have been featured in some of their leaflets and posters. An independent film company also filmed me for a documentary, but this has never been shown. I even agreed to meet a writer by the name of Pete Moore who was putting together a book.

I met Pete off the train from London at King's Lynn Station and suggested we find a quite café where we could talk about me. We walked the short distance into town and found a great little coffee house, Pete had his voice recorder with him and he asked me just to talk about my life and answer a few questions that he might put to me. We sat there for over an hour just talking. It was good as, I had so much to tell him. By the end of our meeting we walked back to the station and he told me that he would let me know when the book would be published, and that I would be getting a copy. The book is called 'Being Me'; What It Means To Be Human'. To read something that's been written about you was quite strange especially when it extends to nine pages.

Another spin-off from my voluntary work with the organisation has been public speaking events. In the summer of 2004 I had a telephone call out of the blue from a friend who lives at Terrington St. Clement in Norfolk. I have known Janet Flowers for several years through her husband Richard. Richard and his father Ted had been farmers in that area of Norfolk where I lived and were customers who came into my mum and dad's pub at Clenchwarton. Janet telephoned me just by chance to ask if I might be able to do a public speaking event at Terrington St Clement Ladies Club. I said that I wasn't too sure about doing anything like this, I had never done so before; Janet asked if I would think about it. I mulled this idea over in my mind for several days. As a youngster I had never been one to stand up in front of anyone to speak, not even to say my name, as I had a terrible fear of doing such things in case it brought attention to myself. Having thought about this though, I soon realised that it might be a good idea as it would bring the issues forward into the thoughts of other people, especially individuals who are facing life with disfigurement each day.

There are lots of things in my life that I was never allowed to do, but there are loads of things that I have done that no-one will ever get the chance to take part in so I have been blessed. I am truly grateful for this wonderful life that has been given to me. Just because you are born a little different from anybody else, it doesn't mean to say that you can't have what you want out of life. I must of course thank James Partridge and Changing Faces for helping to shape my life. James has been such a great inspiration to me, and since being involved with this charity it has made life much more positive than I could have ever imagined. They are all very special people at the charity office and I can never repay what they've given to me.

We endeavour to raise as much money by donations for Changing Faces as possible in order to bring their help to other people who are not able come to terms with their conditions. If you feel that you might like to help the charity in some way, please click on any of the highlighted links within this chapter and it will take you through to the organisation's website. You can also go to the Changing Faces website below for more information.

www.changingfaces.org.uk

Any help at all will be greatly appreciated and if you feel like fundraising yourself there's always lots of way to do this. Why not try a Sky Dive, a Bungee Jump or perhaps even run the London Marathon. These are just a few ideas but I'm sure you'd have great fun doing them.

My Wonderful Life

I do hope that after reading the last few chapters of this book you will see how I have grown in great strength from those early days. I was such a shy little lad throughout those early years, right through school and up until the late eighties, I would let just about anybody walk all over me as I was frightened for fear of any ridicule, but as the years have gone by my self esteem seems to have grown so incredibly beyond belief, I have this wonderful feeling of fulfillment! Let me assure you that as every day goes by it just gets better and better, this powerful feeling gave me the ability to actually go out and stand up in front of people to do my public speaking events, to raise awareness for people who suffer from some kind of disfigurement or other.

I believe the real reason that I am the way I have become has been mainly from the support of my parents, my family, my very dear friends and of course the wonderful help that was given by Changing Faces. All of these people have been there when I needed them most, they have always backed me up throughout my life. My looks have been a blessing in disguise and that it was something that was truly meant to be. I feel that my disfigurement has been more of a help to me than a hindrance, I do hope that through all of this I may have helped other people to be strong too. If my strength has helped just one person in this life, I feel that I may have achieved something!

Please be strong, and please understand that you are no different from anybody else in this whole wide world. We have all been put here for a reason, and I'm trying my very hardest to make a small impact in this life. We are here for just a short time, go and enjoy it, make every day count.

HENRY & ARTHUR'S TRACTION ENGINE LIST

This Traction Engine list has been provided for me by a really lovely old gentleman by the name of Godfrey Sturgeon. Godfrey has told me that these lists were compiled by using some of the other well known Traction Engine enthusiasts such as Alan Duke, Bill Smith and Ronald Clarke but these lists can never be complete as some are different from others. When Henry first started threshing he would for certain have used Portable Engines, and then went on to Tractions.

Henry Bird, and by 1911, Arthur Bird of Vicarage Road, Great Hockham.

Burrell. No 430. 10HP. New 22nd November 1868. At Smithfield Show 1868

New to Henry Bird, later on to John Bird. Sparham

Burrell. No 760. 6HP Single Cylinder. New 8th September 1877. Gear Drive, 2 speeds, Differential, Winding Rope Drum Crossed Steerage Chains. Went back to Charles Burrells, Thetford

Burrell. No 787. 8HP Single Cylinder, Chain Drive, 2 Speeds, Spring Mounted, New September 1878. New to Henry Bird

Burrell. No 1179. 7HP. Single Cylinder. New 11th August 1885. New to Henry Bird

Burrell. No 1436. 8HP (Bill Smith) (7HP. Ronald Clark). New 2nd October 1889, According to Ronald Clark. New to Henry Bird, August 1889, According to Bill Smith. By august 1914 with Beeby Bros, Remstone Notts. 2 Speeds, Spring Mounted, Single Cylinder

Burrell. No 2348. 7HP Single Crank Compound, Spring Mounted. New January 1901. New to Vavasseur, Kilverston Hall, Thetford (N.C.C. No 355) by 1919 to Arthur Bird. Still owned in 1943

Burrell. No 2378. 7HP Single Crank Compound, New 1901, by 1934 from Arthur Clarke. Swaffham. New to A. Hall. Ringstead. Henry Bird, later Arthur Bird, Hockham

Burrell. No 2750. 7HP Single Crank Compound, new May 1905. to Bird's in 1926, from George Thurlow, Stowmarket. Back to G. Thurlows in 1931. Reg No CF4378

Burrell. No 3331. 6HP DE TE Single Crank Compound Devonshire Type. New to Arthur Bird. 16th September 1911. Reg No AH6394. Still owned in 1943

Burrell. No 3420. 7HP Single Crank Compound. Reg AH 5607 New 1912. Spring aft. New to Saxton Noble. Wretham Hall. Next to Sir. John Dewrance, Wretham Hall. By September 1938 to Arthur Bird. by 1953 with Arthur Phoenix, Thetford. Then later by Minns of Carbrooke. Next to George King of Hingham who sold it in 1962 to J Wright of Scarning, who had it by 1968. Then sold to Freddie A Brown, also of Hingham. According to Bill Smith's list it went to William Hammond of Aldborough, Norfolk. Then sold to Paul Haistead in 2003 who started refurbishment but unfortunately died 2006 before it could be finished. Then sold to Norman Millet of Pulham Market, Diss, Norfolk who finished restoring the engine

Burrell. No 3818 6HP Single Crank Compound. Spring Mounted. New to Arthur Bird, 1st September 1919. Reg No 6393. To Arthur Phoenix, Thetford. Before 1921 Norfolk C.C. No 972

Garrett. no 34702. 5 Ton Tractor, Double Crank Compound of 1925. In 1937. ex Caulkett, Clare, Suffolk. By 1950 with Sid Hunt, Filby, Norfolk

Ransomes, Sims & Jefferies. No 39133. 5 Ton Tractor. New 9/1928 DCC

2 Threshing Sets in 1918

ONE LAST NOTE

I do hope that you enjoyed reading my book, and if so please could you leave a favourable review on the **Amazon** website for me?

Thank you for your time.

With kind regards

David Bird

Printed in Great Britain
by Amazon